T0157122

Clear Englebert's other books

Feng Shui Demystified

Bedroom Feng Shui

Feng Shui for Hawaii

Feng Shui for Hawaii Gardens

FENG SHUI

FOR

RETAIL STORES

CLEAR ENGLEBERT

iUniverse, Inc.
Bloomington

FENG SHUI FOR RETAIL STORES

Copyright © 2013 Clear Englebert.

All rights reserved. No part of this book may be used or reproduced by any means, graphic, electronic, or mechanical, including photocopying, recording, taping or by any information storage retrieval system without the written permission of the publisher except in the case of brief quotations embodied in critical articles and reviews.

iUniverse books may be ordered through booksellers or by contacting:

iUniverse
1663 Liberty Drive
Bloomington, IN 47403
www.iuniverse.com
1-800-Authors (1-800-288-4677)

Because of the dynamic nature of the Internet, any web addresses or links contained in this book may have changed since publication and may no longer be valid. The views expressed in this work are solely those of the author and do not necessarily reflect the views of the publisher, and the publisher hereby disclaims any responsibility for them.

ISBN: 978-1-4759-8580-1 (sc)
ISBN: 978-1-4759-8581-8 (e)

Front and back cover design by Rick Mears

Photography and drawings by Steve Mann

Printed in the United States of America

iUniverse rev. date: 5/22/2013

TABLE OF CONTENTS

DEDICATION

This book is dedicated to the owners and managers of independent, locally-owned stores and regional chain stores— real businesses with real storefronts and regular hours— people who are in it for the long haul.

INTRODUCTION

Retail success depends on having the right merchandise, priced right, and being sold by the right staff. It depends on being open in an accessible and noticeable location. These things attract chi. Chi in feng shui is energy, of any kind. Customers are a form of chi energy, coming into your store, giving you money, and leaving with a smile. Money is also a form of chi energy—one that feeds your store and keeps it going by paying bills.

Life in the modern world is faster than life was a few generations ago. Make it *easy* for people to find your store open, and to find what they want to buy. Make it *fast* for the customer to complete their purchase and be on their busy way. Your competition is increasingly from the internet. An internet store is a tool, but a physical store is an *experience*—make it a happy one; therein lies your triumph over internet competition.

GETTING THE YANG OF IT

Yin and yang are ways of describing energy, just as negative and positive describe energy.

A positive retail experience is **yang**. Yang is active and alive, while yin is inactive or dead. **Retail stores are the most yang type of structures** that people build. Mausoleums are the most yin. Homes and offices are between those two extremes, with offices being more yang than homes—but nothing is as yang as a *happening* store. Stores are yang because of the *movement of many people* and the *transactions* that happen. Stores are less affected by some problems that would be very weakening for a yin home. Their *active vitality* is a feng shui cure in and of itself—yang is stronger and yin is weaker—and that strength overcomes many feng shui concerns.

The home should be more restful and the store should be more active. Don't apply the advice in this book to your home, except for Chapter 9.

Movement is very yang. A common retail term is *turns*, which implies activity and refers to the number of times an item sells over a given period of time. Turns can also refer to the number of times that items have sold in a particular location. How many times has the active energy of a customer reached onto that shelf, picked up an item, *and then bought it*? The more movement the better—it ultimately means more money. The word *turns* encapsulates the yang essence of retail stores. Every day should move the store forward. The yang-ness of retail calls for the effective, energetic use of every moment.

A yin/yang chart that applies to retail stores is on the next page.

Retail Yin/Yang Chart

Some of the concepts *that apply to retail* are divided into yang and yin like this:

Yang	Yin
Simple	Complicated
Clean	Dirty
Public	Private
Known	Mysterious
Certainty	Doubt
Light	Dark
Sooner	Later
Quick, Fast, Prompt, Busy	Slow
Movement	Stillness
Strong, Powerful, Increasing	Weak, Vulnerable, Decreasing
Bigger	Smaller
Sharp or Shiny	Dull
Hard	Soft
Sound	Silence
Awake	Sleep
Alive	Dead, Inert
On	Off
Open	Closed
Expansive, Wide	Tight, Narrow
Positive	Negative
Yes	No
Bright, Focused, Alert	Dim, Fuzzy, Scattered
Visible	Hidden
First	Last
Present or Future	Past
Fresh	Worn, Stale, Musty
Crisp	Rumpled, Wrinkled
New	Old
Original, Innovative	Hackneyed
Lively, Energetic, Flowing	Tired, Sluggish, Clogged
Interesting	Boring
Distinct, Specific, Unmistakable	Unclear, Vague
Neat, Exacting	Sloppy

CURES: REAL AND SYMBOLIC

When you encounter a feng shui problem there are two kinds of cures: real and symbolic. **Real cures** are best for most retail situations because you know exactly what kind of chi energy you want to attract to your store—*human beings.* We really do know what attracts the eye—it's been studied quite thoroughly. We also know the techniques that create satisfied customers. And attracting customers once is not good enough; you need to keep *attracting them back again.*

Symbolic cures are used when there is a feng shui concern about the physical shape or layout of the store or the buildings around it and *you cannot change the situation.* Usually a small object, such as a mirror, crystal, or red dot is used to symbolically change a problematic situation. No magic, just a *symbol,* and you *say out loud* what the object is symbolizing. Use your own words and state your purpose when doing symbolic cures. Personally, I think you are addressing your angels and they need to hear your intention spoken out loud. You don't have to say or think about those words again, but you do need to keep the object clean.

CHAPTER 1   NAME & NUMBER

NAME

The name of the store is important to your store's success because it plays a very yang role. The name is the *first thing* that many people will hear or read before they have physically come into your store. Being first is a yang quality.

The store's name should be two to four syllables. Five syllables is sometimes okay, but the more than five is not a good idea. Years ago I went into a restaurant in San Francisco and had a wonderful meal. I told the owner (who was also the waiter) that he should change the name of his restaurant from Org Vegan to something catchier. He asked if I had a suggestion and I said, "Raw." That enterprising young man, Juliano, went on to name his very successful restaurant and book *Raw*. I seldom recommend that retail stores use a one-syllable name, partly because it can sound confusing over the telephone. (The energy of a restaurant is quite different from the energy of a store and different feng shui rules apply.) A one-syllable name is *too* yang for most retail stores. It's best to have at least two syllables—it's more welcoming and generally helps to clarify what your store is about. Some part of the name of the store should *explain* what kind of merchandise you carry. Questionability is a yin characteristic as compared to clarity, which is more yang.

If a catchy name doesn't easily come to mind, I recommend *POP: Stand Out in Any Crowd* by Sam Horn. She addresses the issue of business names in great detail. The perfect name for your store will probably come to mind while you're reading *POP*. See Recommended Reading.

If the name of the business is two words, it will sound more harmonious and lyrical if one of the words has an odd number of syllables and the other word has an even number of syllables. (This is also true for people's names.) If you make the name of your store a joy to say, people are *primed* to love it.

Don't choose a name that is:

- difficult to pronounce
- confusing
- spelled uniquely.

Beware that some names are commonly spelled differently, such as sun and son. Avoid *all* possibilities of confusion and you will have maximized opportunities for chi energy (customers and their money) to find your store.

There should be only one name for the business. It amazes me that I should have to state something so basic, but I've been to businesses that had signs in front with more than one business name. That's horrible—it's confusing and turns people off. You'll never know how many people it turns off because they won't come into your shop in the first place.

It's best to avoid the *arcane* in retail. Don't use Shoppe, or

Olde. Don't have Ltd. at the end of your store's name, as if you expect people to say the word "limited," which I hope you don't because to say that is *limiting* to your store's success. Don't have the amateurish word Enterprises as the last word of the store name—it adds plenty of syllables but they aren't clarifying anything. Plain and simple is yang, and that's what's best in retail. You have to go out of your way to be arcane, and the result is usually too cutesy.

Unless you own the real estate, don't name your store after its *street location*. What if Elm Street Emporium loses its lease and has to move to Oak Street? You can't predict the future, so don't limit possibilities by imagining that your store can only exist at its current location. However, if you *own* the property, you (in a sense) own part of the street, and promoting the recognition of *your street's name* is often to your advantage.

It's a great advantage to have a store name that evokes comforting, familiar, or pleasant memories for the customer. Don't use a name that could be offensive to people who might otherwise be happy to spend money in your store. Any name can *sound* harsher or more pleasant, depending on the speaker's facial muscles and which syllables are accented. More information on how words are spoken and heard is in Chapter 3 under Telephone.

The *spoken* name of a business is a special focus in Jes Lim's *Feng Shui for Business & Office*. See Recommended Reading.

NUMBERS

I practice Landform School feng shui, which teaches that *where* you are is more important than what *number* you are. Landform School is concerned with shapes, much more basic than the abstract concept of a number. Lucky numbers have no place in the feng shui I practice.

The noble number **four** is considered to be not a lucky number by some people whose first language is Cantonese, because it sounds similar to their word for death. English doesn't have *any* rhyming number names that play into superstitions. All numbers are equally good as far as I'm concerned. Find good symbolism in whatever numbers your store has, the numbers visible on the street or numbers dialed from a telephone. Personally, I like the number four because it feels grounded, complete, and solid, like *four-square*.

I don't use numerology in my own life, but there are **four lucky numbers** in Compass School feng shui. They are **3**, **6**, **8**, and **9**. Do with them as you like.

Street Address

Be grateful for whatever numbers are your street address. Be grateful you *have* a street address. It means you're still in business. Make those numbers extremely **visible**—directly over the front door is perfect. Catch the *most* chi energy from the street; let *anyone* looking for your address find you. Not only customers, but emergency first responders can find you easily if you ever need them.

Always place your address numbers in a horizontal row. Never place the numbers in a vertical line. Address numbers in a vertical line are read from top to bottom. That directs energy downward, which is not a favorable direction to move energy.

5371

5
3
7
1

Correct   **Incorrect**

Outside address numbers should read across, not down.

Fig. 1.1

If you are in a historic building and therefore cannot relocate address numbers that are to be read going down, don't add new numbers going horizontally. Honor what you have, and make the vertical numbers look as nice as possible. That can involve carefully taking down the old metal numbers and boiling the heck out of them. If you keep the numbers in plenty of boiling water all the old layers of paint will eventually soften and separate from the metal, which is left unharmed. It can take a while, but you've used no chemicals and haven't scratched old historic metal. If you can choose the new paint color of the numbers be *very bold*—as bold as your neighborhood will allow. Consider using a bright, rich **red**—readable and noticeable. If the old metal numbers turn out to be solid brass, don't paint them; just consider yourself blessed and keep them shiny. When placing the numbers back where they were originally, put the tiniest touch of red paint on the back of the number—a *super-small* dot. Make the intention stronger by saying out loud something like: "You are being placed horizontally."

Red is a symbolic cure and it means *new blood—fresh situation.* Red is commonly used in feng shui for making a symbolic change when no physical change is possible. Even if the front side of the number is already painted red, it's a good idea to put the dot of red on the back side just before putting the numbers up in a vertical orientation. That way you are adding the dot of red *just before* the numbers are reattached to the wall and the intention is vitally in the mind *and being said out loud* during the time that the numbers are being re-screwed to the building. Say your intention out loud *once per number* that is being reattached.

Telephone Number

Your telephone number should have the same prefix as the other stores in your area. If your store has a toll-free number, don't have *just* a toll-free number, have a *local* number as well. It's best to have a land line with your local phone company. I don't recommend having a store with only a cell phone.

The actual number should be easy to remember, so having *repeated numbers* is very advantageous. That makes it *easier* for chi energy to find you. Having repeated numbers *transposed* and in different combinations can be confusing and have a *back-and-forth* energy that does not indicate progress.

Don't have a phone number that spells words, unless you also write the numbers out in your promotional material and on business cards. More information about business cards is at the beginning of Chapter 8.

CHAPTER 2   LOCATION & EXTERIOR

Success begets success—and failure follows failure, so beware of locations where:

- the *immediately previous* store failed
- the location has a *history of failed stores*
- the *immediately previous* store had a poor reputation
- the location has a *history of stores with poor reputations.*

If the immediately previous store failed, but the location doesn't have a repeated history of failed stores, then the location might be fine, but you should definitely do a *cleansing* of the space in a very complete way. You can do that yourself or you can find someone who is experienced in sage smudging. Sage smudging is my preferred method of cleansing a building. My own experience, as well as that of other people I've met, has verified its efficacy. See Smudging in the Glossary.

Questionable locations are best avoided. That *uncertainty* is quite yin. Of course there are exceptions, such as when you feel an area of town is on the verge of resurging. Retail is what moves culture along. Energetic shops can help rejuvenate an older neighborhood through the people they attract.

Locations near large bodies of water can be questionable, unless the business caters primarily to tourists. People don't *live* on those large bodies of water, so in the circumference around your store there is less opportunity to harvest the chi energy that your store needs to survive. Fish markets are the obvious exception.

If possible get a location that allows you to put some merchandise outside. This is not appropriate for all stores, but the stores that do use some sidewalk space for sales are making money on space that otherwise wouldn't produce income. Nothing looks as *fresh* or says OPEN more effectively than merchandise *outside* your front door. Your store is then actively *fishing* in the stream of passersby. I'm referring to carts or racks that are rolled out in the morning and rolled back inside at closing time.

If your store is in a previously residential building, remove most, if not all, of the interior walls and replace them with support posts and beams. Get the necessary permits and do it to code and make the interior look standard retail. That yang declaration will overcome years of history as a yin building—a home. Certain businesses are already quite yin in nature:

- Antique shops
- Gift shops
- Bookstores

These businesses are yin because they involve looking at lots of little things, and they are generally quiet inside. These stores can put to use the different small rooms of an ex-house and still display their merchandise properly and logically.

PARKING

If you expect most of your customers to arrive by driving, then convenient parking is a must for the location. The feng shui symbolism of parking is simple: The potential customer (chi energy) has a huge object they must safely park before they can come inside and spend money (a different kind of chi energy). The mouth of a store is the place where the energy that sustains the store enters. Traditionally, this is the front door. But if your store has its own separate parking lot, the mouth begins at the place where a customer drives in. The main idea is to let your customer easily *know where to park*. Your potential to successfully attract chi is strongly tied to the accessibility of parking.

The message of the parking area should be *we care*. The parking area must be patrolled at least once a day to pick up litter. This is a must. Also be on the lookout for weeds and dead plants. Do this even if you have a shared parking area and none of the other stores accepts responsibility for patrolling it. A car is a very valuable possession—a customer *must* feel confident about where it is parked.

In a perfect world, parking would not be an issue because convenient mass transit would bring the customers close to your store. In the real world, not every store is blessed with nearby mass transit. A nearby, safe parking garage is a great advantage.

When you or your employees are working at the store, don't take the best parking spaces in your lot. Park your car in a relatively unused part of the parking lot. And if the parking lot is fairly large, don't park in exactly the same parking space every day. The *change* of using a different parking space has a yang, *enlivening* effect in an unused area of the lot.

Stores in urban areas need brighter lighting in their parking lots than suburban stores. Perceived safety is most important.

ELECTROMAGNETIC FIELDS (EMFs)

The final thing about location is actually the first thing to check for. Get your hands on a gaussmeter and check the level of electromagnetic fields (EMFs) in the building. Most freestanding buildings have no elevated EMFs, but shops that are crowded together in dense neighborhoods can sometimes have *very* high EMFs. *Certain* electrical wires and devices have magnetic fields around them that are amazingly strong—so strong that you shouldn't spend much time there, otherwise you're running an increased risk of developing cancer. **Test any potential store location for high EMFs.**

I consulted for a potential store location in Honolulu's Chinatown. I didn't consider the EMFs until near the end of the consultation when we were discussing cash register placement. I turned on my gaussmeter and no place in the store had an acceptably low level of EMFs. I just continued out the door and kept checking my gaussmeter. All the neighboring stores had very high EMFs, and the situation continued that way for several blocks. I got some very curious looks from shopkeepers and people around me, but no one kicked me out, even when I went into a restaurant. Occasionally there would be an anomaly, one location with zero EMFs. I assumed the whole problem had something to do with buried electric lines in that part of the city.

I learned a lot from that consultation, and I now check EMFs at the *beginning* of a consultation. I was ready to give my okay on the location, but because of the high EMFs, I had to say no. They agreed, especially because their young children would spend their after-school time in the store. EMFs affect children more severely than adults.

Electromagnetic fields can be measured with gaussmeters. Gaussmeters were not needed for feng shui in ancient China because electrical devices hadn't been invented. I use a Trifield Meter from AlphaLab—the kind most cardiologists use. If you have a cardiologist friend, you could possibly borrow theirs for a few hours. (I hesitate to say this in a book for independent stores, but Amazon sometimes has other gaussmeters at amazingly low prices.)

In my experience, electronic security gates do not have high EMFs *around* the gate, only *within* the gate. No one should stand within a security gate for long periods of time. I can't imagine why someone would want to.

There is no symbolic cure for being in an area of high electromagnetic fields. *You simply shouldn't be there* for long periods of time. The cancers caused by high EMFs can take a couple of decades to develop, but please take these situations seriously—your life and future health are at stake. A sheet of solid metal is the only thing that stops EMFs. There are gimmicky devices that are sold to neutralize high EMFs—some you wear, some you stick on things. They are all bad science— expensive bad science.

EXTERIOR COLOR

The best colors for the exterior of your building (if your store is in a freestanding building) and your sign outside are **red** and **yellow** (with black for lettering). Be cautious of using the greens and browns of nature—those are camouflage colors and they can hide your store. Stores need to *stand out* and be noticed. If you can't stand out physically, you'll need to use color to stand out. Even if your store sells natural products and things related to nature, use bright colors on your outside sign.

You have a very brief time to grab eyeballs as people are busily going past your store. *Color* can grab eyeballs—use it. Even blue should be used with great caution because the sky is blue, so our eyes are very accustomed to seeing that color. However, the right shade of blue can be quite arresting depending on what colors are seen around it. The right color is one that does not predominate on neighboring buildings and stores. If the stores around you are already using reds and yellows, you'll need to pick a color that is different from those shades and perhaps use a purple or an orange. Never use a fluorescent color on any permanent exterior signage.

If you get to decide the outside paint color of your store—oh, lucky you! Don't waste that opportunity on white or some blah color. Chi energy has *eyeballs*—grab them. Be as bold as you are capable of being, and then some. However, the color of the outside of your store should look lovely—not garish, so no fluorescent colors. You have to be sensitive to your neighborhood, and in many cases the neighborhood has already decided which colors are drab enough for their liking. If there are no restrictions on the paint color of the outside of your building, then go for it! Use color to really stand out. But interior store colors are a very different matter; see Chapter 3 for those suggestions.

If a trim color is called for—oh, happy day! Your store gets to *sing* harmony. Put two lovely colors *together* and people can't help but smile. That smile is a sure sign that you are attracting chi energy.

Whatever the exterior color of your store, it must never be in obvious need of a new paint job. Don't have peeling paint on the exterior. Repaint *before* it gets that bad.

The **roof color** of any building should not be blue because that signifies money trouble. Blue symbolizes water, and water symbolizes money. A blue roof says that money is flowing *away from* your business. Any color other than blue is fine. If the roof is already blue, put a crystal up high somewhere in your store to symbolize the dispersing of the blue roof energy before it affects your business.

Signage

There must be a strong contrast between the shade of the lettering and the shade of the background—one should be light and the other should be dark. Don't ever make the background color and the lettering color the same shade of brightness. Some people cannot read green and red right next to each other (especially of the same brightness)—if one color is the background and the other color is the lettering.

If glitter (especially the large-size glitter that is used in boat paint) is possible on your sign and *appropriate for your store*, go for it. For glitter the size of boat paint, a boat painting shop has to do the painting for you, and it won't be cheap—but it *will* be distinctive. I used to enjoy watching one particular soft-drink billboard. It had a blue background and four huge red letters, and all the color came from circles of metallic plastic that were raised on nailheads to be a few inches above the billboard surface. The colors moved and actually *showed* the passing of a small breeze. It was mesmerizing because it used the natural breeze to create the motion.

Motion does indeed work to get people's attention, but it must be used with great caution. Being *garish* is not an appropriate way to be bold. The multitude of flapping triangular banners at used car dealerships are never appropriate for retail stores. Now if your store happens to sell those banners, well go ahead and let the world know. The problem with *lots* of small moving things outside is that the *entire effect* is too yin. Even though there's motion, the fact that it's coming from *many sources* gives it a yin feeling of confusion, not a yang feeling of focus.

The lettering on your sign should be bold or fat, without looking obnoxious or unreadable. Fat equals abundance in feng shui, and bold letters declare, "Bring it on—there's room for lots of prosperity in this store." Slender or skinny letters say, "There's not much ability to absorb prosperity." Most lettering should be done in block letters, but if cursive or longhand lettering is used for a *handwritten* look, you must read *Change Your Handwriting, Change Your Life* by Vimala Rodgers. It's the final book in Recommended Reading.

San serif lettering is preferred for retail signage because it is simpler and therefore more yang. If you mix serif and san serif fonts in your signage or publicity, make sure the lower part of the small "g" of each font looks similar. If you do your own graphic design on your sign, or anywhere related to your store, read *The Non-designers Design Book* by Robin Williams. It would also be wise to expose yourself to a huge variety of fonts. Spend some time looking at books of fonts. Whether it is distinctive or plain, the font you use *must* be easy to read. Never use more than one background color directly behind lettering because that makes the words harder to read.

Obey the sign ordinance in your area, but go for the maximum size allowable. Don't use a banner sign (with grommets)—it screams *temporary* as if that's all your business will ever be. Have your permanent exterior sign painted on *wood or metal*, which are preferable to plastic because they convey the message, "This store will stay, because it will prosper here." Your permanent sign should be up by the day your store first opens. Banners are best used to announce the *coming* of your store to a new location, but *by your first open day* have a permanent sign. A grand opening with only a banner sign for the business name is never an auspicious beginning for a store.

It's usually best to spell out words fully in signage (inside and outside the store) rather than abbreviate. Spelled-out words leave no room for doubt about the message. They convey a subtle message to your customers that you are careful. Signage is not texting, and should not resemble it. (The only abbreviation that is acceptable has to do with the price of the item, for example: "$8 per doz." is better than "Eight dollars per dozen.") A local store recently added this to their sign: WHSE. Does that mean warehouse or wholesale? This is greeting chi energy with a question mark. Ambiguity invites *nothing*!

Sometimes a store inherits the sign of the previous store, which they are expected to paint over. That's fine unless the sign has an unusual shape that was specially designed for another store. In that case, you must make your lettering and decoration *fit* the sign as if it were made for *your* store. Otherwise, there will be an awkward look that won't invite as much chi energy as is due.

If your store is open in the evening, your outside sign must be well lit. Neon is a very powerful kind of signage, and therefore quite yang. It screams *substantial* if only because it's a substantial investment in the first place. If your sign is neon people expect that your store will stay around for decades, enriching the community. *Beware of moving neon lights* however—they can easily look tawdry—as can any moving light. Be cautious and classy if you're using any moving lights at night. Oh, they attract energy all right—but because they're *so noticeable* they can attract more than their share of the-lowest-common-denominator kind of energy. The familiar blue and red neon OPEN signs are fine for stores that are open after dark, because they do indeed attract chi energy, *and* they leave no room for ambiguity.

FRONT DOOR

The entrance is the *mouth* of your store, where the energy that sustains your store enters. As soon as your store is noticeable, the *door* (or the area around your door, if the door is recessed) should be noticeable. The ideal is to *catch the eye*—unmistakably! Never let a new customer wonder even for a moment how to get inside your store.

I helped one client pick her store's front door color when I bumped into her at a big hardware store. I had originally suggested red, but later reflected that red wouldn't stand out properly against the color of the building, which is purple. When we were still three aisles away from the paint aisle, I said, "I see the right shade of yellow." She said, "What are you talking about?" I said, "I can see a big yellow paint chip from here." We walked directly to that chip and I handed it to her. Lavender Moon Gallery's front doors are that rich yellow color today. Purple and yellow go together well.

Make the outside of your front door *red*, if you can. Don't paint the inside of the door red unless your door is kept open and pushed outward most of the time. If you cannot make it red, use any other bright color. If you do not control the front door color, perhaps you can have a red rolling cart that goes outside near the door when your store is open, or put a brightly colored object outside near the door.

If there are plants outside near your door, the plants must not be thorny or have leaves that are sharp, stiff, and spikey. Those plants, in that location, greet chi energy with swords and daggers—not friendly! Instead, the plants near the door should have round or rounded leaves, and if the leaves are fat (such as those of jade plants and many sedums) the symbol is that *abundance* will roll in your door. I used to visit a store that sold feng shui-related merchandise and there was a small garden space outside. The owner had planted a few pointed-leaf succulents in the area and surrounded them with pebbles. The pebbles said "Barren—nothing grows here" and the pointed plants were unfriendly. When I mentioned the store to people they always had the same comment—sparse merchandise and not a friendly reception. The store didn't last long.

In older buildings, an air conditioner is sometimes directly over the front door. This is not ideal because it represents a looming object over people's heads. But unless you own the store there's little you can do about it. If moisture drips onto the sidewalk outside the front door, that's even worse. Once again, what can you do? If moving the machine is not an option, use a symbolic cure. Hang a very small crystal from the air conditioner to symbolically disperse the harsh, awkward energy of the machine. The crystal should be clear and can be quite small—a fourth of an inch in diameter is fine. If the crystal is *too* noticeable, someone might rip it down. When you hang it say out loud that its symbolic purpose is to disperse the energy of the air conditioner, so that it doesn't adversely affect people coming and going through your doors. You could also use a mirror to symbolically push the machine further away. Glue a very small mirror to the bottom of the air conditioner (with the shiny side facing up) and say your intention out loud. You don't have to do both cures—one is enough.

Sometimes stores have more than one front door, but one of them is permanently blocked—perhaps even having the back of a display fixture visible from the outside. The first thing to do is make the unused front door look very nice from the outside. And there must be a sign with an arrow pointing to the actual entrance to the store. A sign should be with the arrow, saying, "Use other entrance" or similar words. If possible, make the unused door look *less* like a door and more like a wall or display window. If you do a good job of visually *erasing* the door, you will not need an arrow or sign.

Any door, anywhere in your store, that is blocked and never used as a door any more suggests *blocked opportunities*, which is something you definitely don't want in a business. Put a tiny red dot on the door in a discreet place and say out loud, "You are not a door anymore. You're now the wall." or words to that effect. Once again, the power of the color red is often used in feng shui to symbolize *new blood*. The red is symbolizing that a change is made, when a real physical change is not feasible. Anything that is broken in your store, that you cannot get repaired immediately, should have a dot of red on it. When placing the red dot say, "You're fixed." The red dot can be a tiny red sticky dot that is sold in office supply stores. It can be a dot of red paint or even nail polish. The dot can be as small as a pinhead.

The direction of the swing of the front door is important. If it opens only outward, the symbol is that you are repelling the chi energy of people who are trying to enter your store. They have to pull an object away from your store *first thing*. (Things that happen first are very important in feng shui.) If you cannot change the swing direction of a front door that swings only outward, put a dot of red paint on it somewhere very discreet and say something like: "You open inward as well as outward." Also have a PULL sign on the door. The sign should be fairly close to where a person reaches to open the door. The ideal direction for a store's front door to swing is **both directions**. That way a customer can't get it wrong. Your store is saying "yes" to them no matter which way they try to open the door. If a door opens only inward, that's okay (but it's never as good as both directions) because as they enter the store the door is symbolically drawing them in. Be sure to have a PUSH sign on the door. I know of a store whose front doors open in both directions but there's a sign on the outside of the doors saying PUSH. Don't do that at your store.

Don't have a door handle that looks as if it should be pulled, as in Fig. 2.0, when in fact it can only be pushed. When the customer tries to pull the door and it won't pull, their first impression is that the door is locked, and that disturbs their chi energy because they thought you were open. That split second when they do something wrong *first thing* is a powerful disadvantage for a store. In that situation, if you cannot change the kind of handle on the door, at least have a PUSH sign.

This kind of door handle should only be used on a door that can be **pulled** open.

Fig. 2.0

Doors that gently self-close are preferred because the customer doesn't have to continue dealing with the door once they have set foot in your store. Once they are in your store, they're *fresh*. But after the few seconds it takes to close the door they're not quite as fresh.

Outside doormats invite chi energy into your door. Have one if you can—preferably the kind with a rubber edge that lies flat against the sidewalk. The doormat should be red. If everyone around your store has red doormats, then use yellow, which may be harder to find. Don't use a doormat that is smaller than the width of the door. Fig. 2.1 shows an incorrect size and Fig. 2.2 shows a correct size. Double doors need a double-size doormat—nothing smaller.

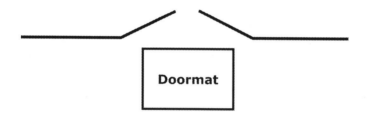

This doormat is too small.

Fig. 2.1

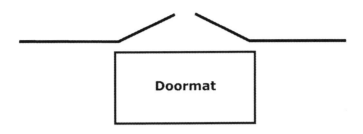

This doormat is the correct size.

Fig. 2.2

A semicircle-shaped mat is never appropriate for *outside* your door, as in Fig 2.3. It symbolizes your wealth *flowing away* from the store. A semicircle shape *inside* your front door is fine because it symbolizes wealth *flowing into* your store, and dispersing throughout the store. The shape resembles the spout of a pitcher. Water symbolizes money and you want that flowing into your store, not out of it. Inside or out, mats at the door are a gracious way to welcome chi energy, and they keep the floor in better condition.

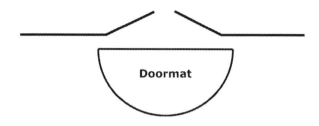

Never use a semicircular doormat **outside** your front door.

Fig. 2.3

WINDOWS & AWNING

Exterior windows that people pass by are almost essential for retail stores. Stores without them are at a *huge* disadvantage. It's almost as if you are not in business at all. A clear glass window lets the chi energy of many potential customers come into your store while they are *still outside*. That sheet of glass is, in a sense, letting you enlarge the size of your store.

If your windows have shelving backed up to them, put posters on the back of the shelves so there's something attractive in the window. Change the posters before they start to fade—that's essential since faded objects are yin and represent the past. Faded window displays can actually *repel* customers. Most items in a display window will fade much quicker than you wish.

Some stores, especially fabric stores, put a tinted plastic film in or on the windows to reduce the fading caused by sunlight. I sympathize with the intention, but I cannot approve of it from a feng shui point of view. Reflective film of any kind must never be used on store display windows or glass front doors. Reflecting the sight of your customers away from your store is the *opposite* of good retail feng shui. Unless you want your store to look like a porno shop, don't use reflective film.

When a store window is tilted outward at the top the visibility into the store is increased, because glare on the glass is reduced to a minimum. Those tilted windows are sometimes found on mid-twentieth-century buildings. Distinctive windows draw the eyes in a way that is irresistible—it's almost impossible *not* to look at them. Reward those eyes with a nice view. When you have distinctive windows, you are under an even greater obligation to keep them clean, with attractive displays and fresh-looking trim paint.

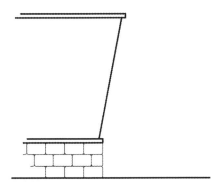

Slanted windows are distinctive and must be kept
very clean and attractive.

Fig. 2.4

Cleaning

The first thing about windows is that they *must* be clean. Even windows that have display cases backed up to them have to be kept clean. Store windows should be cleaned weekly and glass doors should be cleaned daily or several times a day as needed. You'll see increased sales if your store windows look *glossy* on the outside. That gloss is important. It's what people see when they are outside your store wondering whether to go inside. If you *don't* have clean windows, some chi energy *will* pass you by. Dirty windows get noticed, especially when a potential customer is making up their mind as whether or not to *enter* for the *first time*. That's not a small decision, and if you help the person outside your store become the person *inside* your store, you've done something practically *magical*. The true job of your windows is to draw chi energy (people) into your store. So if you have windows—*use them*! They extend your store beyond the limits of the area that you are paying rent on.

Never use a standard blue chemical window cleaner. It is extremely toxic to breathe—*much* more so than most people realize—often the most toxic item in a person's house. Use something more natural than that, such as a standard clean-rinsing liquid made for non-machine dishwashing. Joy Liquid is often recommended by professional window cleaners. Dilute it to the strength of one or two *drops* per gallon of cold water—you do not want *soapy* water! Keep that handy in a spray container for touchups. For  cleaning an entire large window, use a bucket and *drench* the area of glass to be cleaned, applying some friction with a non-linty cloth called a scrubber sleeve that fits over a piece of rigid plastic. Use a large squeegee to dry it. The small squeegees designed for car windows are too small for store display windows. You'll also need a few good cotton drying cloths. Don't use a rag with an unhemmed edge, because it will leave lint on the glass.

The *best* drying cloths are very absorptive cotton. Not all cotton fabric is absorptive; Cannon brand dishtowels are, but they're not cheap and the only source I know is eBay. The blue cleaning cloths that professional janitors (and car mechanics) use are also good. Detailed instructions on window cleaning are in *Spring Cleaning* by Jeff Campbell. Window cleaning equipment is available at any janitorial supply store or through websites such as detroitsponge.com.

Awning

If there is an awning over the outside front of your store, consider yourself blessed and take good care of it. If you can install an outside awning, please do. It attracts chi energy and causes it to linger. The store is physically extending its space in the world. It's growing, and that's ideal. If you can sell merchandise under the awning, *you'll never look back.* People can congregate at your store and enjoy browsing outside. Your awning should stay clean and new-looking, even if you are selling used merchandise beneath it.

Harsh Energy Nearby

Problems can originate from the unfavorable shapes of neighboring buildings, roads, and landform.

A **sharp right angle** of a neighboring building is shown in Fig. 2.6. When the corner of a building *points* at your store, it is as if the point of an arrow is aimed at you. This is called a poison arrow. The cure is a mirror, used as described in the next topic.

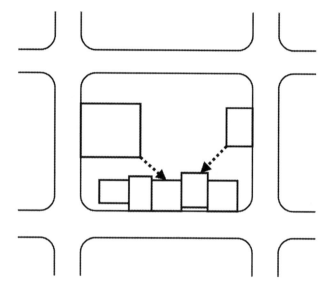

Poison arrows from neighboring buildings affecting two buildings or stores.

Fig. 2.6

A **narrow alley** between two buildings is a problem if it aims at your store as in Fig. 2.7. The alley is like a rifle barrel conducting chi too harshly. The cure, once again, is a mirror.

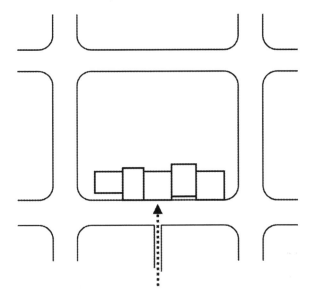

The middle store is being hurt by the harsh energy of the straight line from the alley.

Fig. 2.7

A **T-intersection** can be unfavorable for stores for the same reason. An out-of-control vehicle aimed directly at your store is an unlikely event, but it *seems* more imminent at a T-intersection because many cars are indeed aimed at your store. A physical barrier between your store and the road aimed at it is ideal. Crash-resistant bollards or large architectural planters are examples. The barrier should be very eye-catching and painted red if possible. Any mirror between your store and traffic should never cause a problem with light reflecting in the drivers' eyes. *Very small* mirrors are usually more appropriate when putting them near the height of car headlights. If a mirror could conceivably cause a traffic accident, the mirror is in the wrong place.

A problem of oppression is created if your building is no taller than three floors, and there's a **much taller building** on your block, on your side of the road. Tall buildings across the street are not a problem, unless they are aiming a sharp corner at your building, as in Fig. 2.8. If a very tall building is on your side of the road, on your block, aim a concave mirror at the tall building. However, if there is a tall building directly behind your store the symbolism is good—you've got *strong backing*.

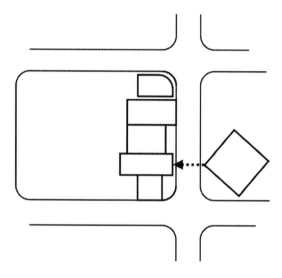

Harsh energy from the corner of a building across the street.

Fig. 2.8

Feng Shui Mirrors

Any sharp or oppressive shape in the neighborhood around your store should be reflected away with a small round mirror. Place the mirror outside your store if you can. Aim the reflective side directly at the problem shape. The different shapes of mirror surfaces are used for particular feng shui purposes. Any mirror used in feng shui should be cleaned occasionally. The *shininess* of the mirror has a lot to do with its effectiveness.

Flat

Small, dime-size flat mirrors are cheaply available at craft stores. They are the kind that most people use as feng shui solutions, because they are so discreet. A flat mirror aims energy directly back at the problem; therefore it must face the problem square on. Use something like double-sided foam tape for padding behind one side of the mirror to adjust where it aims. A flat mirror, of any size, is the only shape that is effective to bring back *missing areas*, which are discussed in Chapters 6 and 9.

Convex

A convex mirror curves outward. It reflects and disperses energy from many directions. They're available where auto supplies are sold.

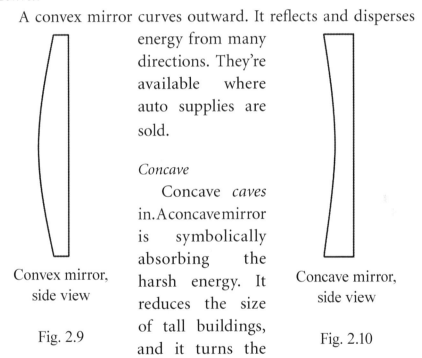

Convex mirror, side view

Fig. 2.9

Concave

Concave *caves* in. A concave mirror is symbolically absorbing the harsh energy. It reduces the size of tall buildings, and it turns the reflected image of the building upside down, saying "You're not important." A concave mirror is almost always appropriate to use outside a building, especially for the problem of neighboring buildings that are so large that they are out-of-scale for the neighborhood.

Concave mirror, side view

Fig. 2.10

Bagua Mirror

A bagua mirror is a feng shui mirror that has eight trigrams from the *I Ching* (arranged in perfectly balanced order) on the frame around the outside. It is primarily for use outside, when you want to push harmful energy away from your store. The bagua mirror is special because of *the frame* around the mirror. The actual mirror surface can be any of the three above shapes that is appropriate for the problem. More information is under Bagua mirror in the Glossary.

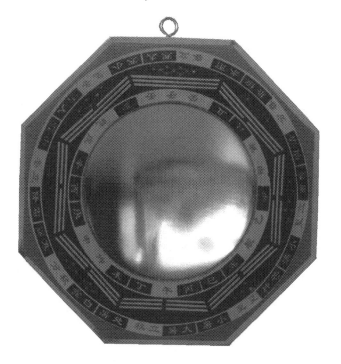

Yang Robustness

Large, active stores with plentiful parking can be strong enough—yang enough—to resist harsh energy in their neighborhood. That's the power of being yang. The more new-looking your store is the more yang it is. This is true even for antique stores. Your merchandise can look weathered but your store itself should look as clean and new as you can keep it.

CHAPTER 3   GREETING CHI ENERGY

The stores that win are those that greet chi energy with a **yes** said firstly, unmistakably, and continually. That's the yang way to do it.

STORE HOURS

Most stores that open at 10:00 a.m. would benefit from opening at 9:30. And many stores that open at 9:30 would be better off opening at 9:00 a.m. Even 8:00 a.m. is not too early for certain stores in certain locations. Depending on the *type* of store, 6:00 a.m. can be a fine opening time. If you find people are waiting for your store to open, the store should be opened earlier—period.

No store should close at 5:00 or 5:30 p.m. At that time there are too many people *who have just gotten off work* who might need to dash into your store on their way home. Don't close before 6:30 or 7:00 p.m. Many stores should be open until 8:00 or 9:00 p.m. 10:00 p.m. is not too late in some city locations, and I've worked in stores that were open until midnight on

Friday and Saturday. If you're having to scoot out a good many shoppers when you close, the store is closing too early. When I worked at Green Apple Books in San Francisco, the store was always open until midnight on Fridays and Saturdays because it's in a neighborhood with lots of good restaurants. The policy was that any woman who worked on that shift was permitted to take a taxi home, and the store would reimburse her.

If you are not open or not answering the phone during the hours that your store is supposed to be open, you are killing your business. Customers are not as forgiving as you might assume or wish. It is unspeakably disappointing to a customer to arrive with a red-hot wallet and find a *locked door*. If your store is tiny and you *have* to go do something while you are supposed to be minding the store—you must hire some trustable *spot labor*. Take your business seriously enough to be *open* if you expect customers to take it seriously enough to spend money there. The only kind of sloppy hours that are allowed, even encouraged, is *opening early and closing late*. Encourage your employees to personally answer the phone before and after your posted business hours. And if that tells you to open a little earlier or close a little later, well do so. Your store will receive money to the degree that you serve people's needs. And if *they* (the public—your potential customers) indicate that you should stretch your hours, then stretch your hours.

If you *must* dash out of the store and close it briefly, don't post a sign saying "Back in ten minutes." No one knows *when* the sign was posted, so it's best to say something like "Back at 10:30."

The sign that displays your hours should simply say HOURS, not HOURS OF OPERATION.

I know of a small bookstore that announced it would be closed for inventory Monday through Friday, on a certain week.

Closing for five days *for inventory* is absurd—it says, "This store is a hobby." One day is the maximum that any store should ever close for inventory—hopefully *not* a day in early January. People are still itching to spend money on January first *if* they can find stores open for them. Most stores can stay open *and* do inventory at the same time. Put up signs announcing that inventory is going on and have all hands on deck. On your inventory day you may need to hire extra help—people who are fast, accurate, and focused. Customers are surprised and charmed to see the inventory happening. But mostly the customers are *grateful* that they are allowed to shop instead of being turned away at the door.

FIRST IMPRESSION

The daily opening of your store declares a party to which anyone and everyone is invited. Make them *all* feel welcome and included. Greeting chi energy well can result in:

- An immediate sale
- A repeat customer
- Someone who gives you good word-of-mouth advertising—the *best kind* of advertising.

Always acknowledge people when they come into your store. Smile and say something quite brief such as "Welcome" or "Hello" or "Let me know if I can help you." Don't say, "How can I help you?" because it's too abrupt. "May I help you?" is a yes-or-no question that runs the risk of getting a negative response. Why make a customer say "No" first thing? Anytime a customer *comes directly to you*, as if to seek help, your best response is a smile and the word "Yes." You essentially are saying, "Yes, I'm available to help you" without their having to ask. Hopefully, none of your staff would dream of saying, "*Can* I help you?" That question indicates the speaker doesn't know English grammar very well. Never have staff that seem to be uneducated.

The **smile** is very important. Roger Axtell, author *Gestures,* says that the smile is the *only* universal gesture that runs no risk of misinterpretation—everyone everywhere understands a smile. Even if you are on the phone, you must acknowledge the new customer who has just entered your store. At least smile and nod at the person.

If you are busy helping another customer and that customer is talking to you—smile, hold up your index finger to the person talking (signifying "Just one second and I'll be right back to you") and say to the new person, "I'll be with you shortly" or words to that effect. Your finger aids in your authority to be *traffic cop* in your store. It helps you manipulate chi energy.

Acknowledging people as they enter will also *greatly decrease shoplifting* because the person is aware that they have been noticed. Say something *brief* because it's best to assume the customer has a busy life. You yourself should have a busy life— and by that I mean that you should be busy doing something (that the store needs done) *when* the customer comes into the store. Only very large big box stores can afford to have an official greeter whose sole job is to greet customers at the door. Any employee of your store should be able to assume the job of greeter by simply *making eye contact* with customers and smiling. This can be done in stores of any size and need not be restricted to the area near the front door. If a customer then asks a question (because you made eye contact), well that's good because you've made it easy for them to get help. Your employees need to very comfortable making eye contact (and smiling).

The greeter should already be on the sales floor or behind the counter. Do not emerge from a back room when the customer enters or the customer will wonder if they are interrupting something else that you would rather be doing. It can even seem like a spider emerging from the hole in their web.

If it is appropriate for your store, put your hands together in gratitude, with a slight bow, when greeting customers. It can also be an appropriate way to express gratitude for a sale, or even to wish a non-buying customer a good day. Non-buying *now* doesn't mean non-buying *in the future*—be equally nice to the customer who just browsed. Express your appreciation to anyone who has come into the store.

Some store owners feel they need a bell sound every time their door opens. Many factors can influence this decision, such as the kind of neighborhood you're in and the number of sales staff on the floor. Avoid having a bell sound if you can safely do so, because it's jarring to the customer who is entering. If you deem a bell sound to be *necessary*, make sure it is gentle and pleasant. Some stores have a sensor system with an abrupt electric buzzer sound when a customer enters. That repels chi energy. Change the electric alert sound to resemble birds chirping or something similarly pleasant. If you have an actual bell hanging from the door, hang the bell from a bracket that is extended from the upper part of the door. Never have bells that just clang and knock against the door, such as those hanging from a doorknob or handle. Don't use a cowbell as the front door bell—it's not pleasant enough. You'll know you have the right sound if some customers inquire where they can buy those nice bells—and your answer should be, "They're right over here."

AMBIENCE

The main ambience your store should have is cleanliness. A dirty, or somewhat dirty, store will not be as successful as it would be if it were clean. Clean is yang, and stores must emphasize yang. When cleaning, be sure to remove any old pieces of transparent plastic tape from *wherever* they may be—windows, register area, walls, or office. The stuck tape represents stuck energy from the past. One of my clients had zillions of bits of tape stuck everywhere in her office. When I asked her about it she said that the previous tenant has taped zillions of things to the walls. I told her they all had to go, and (bless her heart) she did it herself that weekend. That Tuesday she left a message on my telephone saying that already two people had shown up who owed her money from the past—money she never thought she would collect because the bills were over two years old. Not only did the people pay what they owed, they paid *extra* because they felt guilty.

SOUND

Yin is quiet—quiet as a tomb. Tombs are the complete opposite of stores in the yin/yang scale of buildings. A store needs to be yang for it to be profitable. It's *very* good to have recorded music in your store because it makes your store more yang—*sounds* are happening. But no words—no rap, no opera, and no radio. This is true even if your store *sells* opera, rap, or radios. These things interfere with concentration, and are not helpful in any retail environment. You have only *two choices*, but as categories they are huge:

- **Instrumental** or
- **Singing, but *only* in a language that most of your customers don't understand.**

When those special forms of chi energy known as the customers are in your store, let them get *deeply* into the merchandise for sale. People can't concentrate as well when they are hearing broadcast words that have nothing to do with the merchandise they are looking at—*if* they can understand those words. Music allows customers to feel that they are not creating the only sounds in the store. Let your customers think, but also have some privacy when talking.

Keep the volume fairly low. Small speakers throughout the store are best. The worst thing is *speakers that are close to the cashiers*. The recorded music makes telephone conversations more difficult, as well as conversations between the person making a purchase and the cashier. Those two people need to be able to hear each other *very* distinctly.

One of my favorite stores in San Francisco sold large statues and fountains. As soon as you walked in there was the refreshing sound of flowing water. Strolling through the store was an enchanting experience because as the sound of one fountain was left behind another fountain with a different sound was heard. It felt so cleansing and good to be there that it was almost painful to step out onto the sidewalk and hear traffic and city sounds again.

SMELL

Most stores should just smell fresh, with no added scent whatsoever. The more you add scent, the more you will be driving away potential customers who either don't like the same scent that you like or who are allergic to scents in general. If your store has a smell that naturally comes from the merchandise you stock, that's not a problem unless the smell is powerful. Powerful smells are appealing to *some* customers, but not all. You run the risk of driving customers out the door (for fresh air) before they can give you money—*not* a good idea!

Employees should not wear perfume or cologne while on the

sales floor. Those scents turn off as many people as they turn on. A customer won't tell you they are allergic to your perfume, so you'll never know how many sales you've lost. Even in a perfume department, it's best for the employee to have a neutral smell—let the customer pick what they want to smell. Employees should simply look and smell *clean*, and that's sufficient.

The only store that should smell like pets is a pet store. Some customers are attracted to certain pets—and some customers are repelled by them. You'll know about the customers who love your pets, but you won't know about the customers who are allergic to them—they'll quietly leave and shop elsewhere. Keeping any pet (that is not for sale) in your store *is* reducing the chi energy that you harvest—you're getting less money.

COLOR

Bold colors inside a store can confuse chi energy, so *muted* is the keyword here. It is essential that the wall color does not *compete* with the merchandise. Someone may love the merchandise, but they may not like the loud color behind it. They see it along with the image of the item you want them to spend money on, and they may be too influenced by the color to buy the item. A store can look stylish without loud background colors. Make people look at your merchandise, not your walls. Even a paint store should follow this advice. That being said—there are certain stores that can use bold (but not fluorescent) colors *if they compliment the merchandise.* That's the deciding factor about wall color—how does the merchandise look next to the color?

For many stores, there's nothing wrong with using a white that leans a bit toward off-white for the wall color of the sales floor, or some fairly light nondescript color. Feng shui colors for specific types of stores are given on page 82 of Sarah Rossbach's

Living Color, reviewed in Recommended Reading. Not every wall has to be the same color. Small shops often benefit from having the back wall a darker color than the other walls, giving a feeling of depth. Bold, interesting colors can be used to draw customers' attention to certain areas. Just be sure those colors aren't competing with the merchandise. *Stark* white walls are too sterile for most stores, but they are fine for drug stores, which benefit from the association with sterility as long as the white looks clean. White shows dirt quickly so it brings the obligation to be vigilant with cleaning. Off-white to beige colors are warmer and more comfortable to be around. The darker the wall color, the brighter the lighting must be because there is less reflected light.

The ceiling of the sales floor should be white (or a light color) unless it is extremely high in relation to the square footage. In that case it can be a darker color to make it seem lower and thereby help with the feeling that the store has balanced proportions. The floor color should be only so dark as to not quickly show dirt (and therefore *always* look dirty). Many stores have white floors, and they are under the obligation to do the necessary maintenance to keep them looking clean. Dirt is yin; clean is yang.

A yang wall is most basically a **new-looking** wall. There's great *strength* in having yang walls because the walls support the store. Different walls in your store can have different sheens, from matte to glossy. But *the sheen of an individual wall should be consistent* on the entire surface of that wall. An inconsistency in sheen can come with age, use, and repairs. Even pushpin holes should be spackled and painted over. All traces of old tape glue should be removed with something like GooGone. Repaint over scuffs that don't readily clean off. Always keep your walls looking new.

Bathrooms are severely yin because of the moisture. Yellow and beige are good colors for your store's bathroom. Those colors represent earth and in feng shui earth is considered to control water. Light green is also a good color for most bathrooms. The green represents plants that symbolically suck up the excess moisture.

Temperature

A basic tenet of feng shui is *balance,* and having an agreeable temperature in your store is crucial. Especially, your store should not be *too cold* and thereby too yin. Grocery stores are susceptible to being too cold, because of the need to refrigerate merchandise. When that cannot be avoided use warm colors on the walls and tint the ceiling with a warm color. If your store is artificially cooled or heated, do not leave your doors open. Customers notice this *waste* the instant they are at your front door, and it is a turn-off. Stores in an enclosed mall may leave their mall-side entrance open with no loss of goodwill from the customer.

If it's rainy, have a container inside near the door for people to put their umbrellas. It will be seen as courteous by the customers and will help keep your merchandise dry.

Lighting

Dimly lit stores don't do as well as stores with adequate lighting. *Adequate* differs with the type of store. If your merchandise requires a customer to read a label, the lighting must be brighter than a clothing store where there is much to look at but little to read. Some big box stores are overly lit and become so yang that they are uncomfortable to be in, and the bright lighting causes the merchandise to be perceived as cheap and low-quality.

Harsh lighting, such as a spotlight, should never be located so it can shine in customers' eyes. Shine light on the *merchandise*, not the customers!

Incandescent lighting is preferred because there is no flicker in the bulb, as there is with fluorescent and LED bulbs. Halogen bulbs are fine for spotlights. If your store has fluorescent lighting, change the bulbs as soon as some darkness appears at the end of a tube. Otherwise you are wearing out the ballast, which is much more expensive to replace than the bulb. **Dispose of fluorescent light bulbs as hazardous waste.** They contain mercury and should not be broken or put in regular garbage.

It's best to turn off all store lights when the store is closed. Police agree; it's easier to spot a burglary in a dark building. The darkness in your store provides a balance of energies—a time of rest. Likewise don't have exterior lighting that stays on in the daytime. Put such lights on timers and adjust them with the seasons.

EMPLOYEES

Feng shui teaches how to manipulate objects and living things (including people) to accomplish your goals—and the goal in retail is more money in the cash register. The owner or manager needs to manipulate the chi energy of two kinds of people—the customers and the employees.

Employees who regularly interact with the customers must have poise and confidence and treat customers politely. They should be naturally energetic and vivacious, cheerful and buoyant—*or* be willing to do a good job of acting that way when they are on the sales floor. Employees who are helpful, enthusiastic, and knowledgeable (about the store and its merchandise) are your **best assets**. They can build your customer base like nothing else. Employees who can genuinely empathize with a customer are not common and they are *gold*. Some valued employees may be paid more than yourself. Alice Waters, the founder of Chez Panisse restaurant says, "Part of my philosophy is to try to give employees a great quality of life. My guiding principle is to put myself in their place and ask what I would find desirable in a job."

If a person enjoys working with customers it will *show*—it can't help but show. Notice that, and advance that employee as far as they want to go in your business, even to the point of opening and managing a new branch of your store. (Yes, *your* store in more than one location!) Don't bring someone in as a manager if you've already got employees who are capable of handling the work that the position requires. Always hire *up* from within your store. This gives your good employees more incentive to stay.

If two of your employees start a relationship, that's okay. It will undoubtedly raise their chi energy because that tends to happen when someone is in love.

Train your employees correctly and your store is ready to *grow*. Managing employees is best done with positive encouragement, keeping negative comments to a minimum. Retail is detail— don't forget that, and impress it in your employees. If someone isn't willing to pay strict attention to details and lots of them, then that person was not meant for retail employment. Most people *aren't* cut out for retail—don't assume they are. Be careful who you hire and who you retain. Teach your employees to date and sign (or initial) every note they write. Your life will be easier because of it.

All employees should thoroughly understand that their paycheck comes from the *customer*. The owner or manager *signs* the check, that's all. Larger stores have employees who work *only* in back offices, such as bookkeepers. I think it's a good idea to have *every* employee trained to help customers, just in case of an emergency. But *don't* pull your back office staff onto the sales floor if it's *not* an emergency.

An employee should behave the same way when the owner is gone as when they are in the store. To find out if this is happening, you might need to ask a friend to drop in and browse at a time when you're not there. This is especially a good idea when evaluating new employees. If your employees are having a gabfest when you're gone, it's time to take some action. If you encourage gabfests when you're at the store, you are setting a bad example. I was recently called to consult on the feng shui of a doctor's reception room while he was out of town. When I entered the room and went to the reception desk both of the receptionists were on the phone. I waited—knowing full well that they were aware that I was there. Neither of them would look up to make eye contact or smile. I gave up and proceeded to walk around the reception room making notes of my findings and recommendations. I finally left and neither of the receptionists had ever acknowledged me. When I later made my report to the doctor and told him how I was treated, I said that if I had been a potential client, I would have left rubber in his parking lot. He had no idea that his receptionists were so poorly trained and said that he would speak to them immediately. Having someone who is not known to your employees visit your store when you're gone can give you an incredible amount of valuable information.

The people best suited for retail work are those who are physically fit. Regardless of how much a person weighs, they need to be able to move quickly and gracefully in retail. If the retail employee (who works with the public) is a heavy person, they need to be perceived as a very *strong* person. That causes the chi energy of the customers to feel *protected*. Fat as flab has a sluggishness that is not best suited to the yang atmosphere of the retail sales floor. Don't have employees who go around with their mouth open—it looks like the person is sluggish, to say the least. A sluggish look in retail is wrong. A proper retail staff is *quick* and *smart*. When you get staff like that pay them *well* so you keep them.

DRESS CODE

The larger and busier a store is, the more a uniform for employees is needed. The uniform makes it easier for customers to find help. Smaller stores shouldn't need to require uniforms—but shirts, aprons, or badges can be quite helpful in medium-size stores. The badges can be pinned on a person's shirt or worn as a pendant. Dress codes should require that the employees' clothing look clean and crisp (*appropriately* crisp anyway). If your employees have good sense they'll wear appropriate clothes. If they *don't* have good sense, you don't want them working for you. You should deal with that as well as revisiting your hiring process and instruction manual.

Jewelry in facial piercings should be kept to a minimum when an employee is on the sales floor. They are welcome to reinsert their jewelry after work. The time a person is at work isn't a time to say, "Look at me." It's a time for customers to look at merchandise. Simplify things in your customers' minds by allowing them to focus on their shopping. Small-pierced earlobes are acceptable for anyone. It's a different matter if a clerk is wearing a pair of extravagant earrings or conspicuous facial jewelry *and the store sells those earrings or that jewelry.* That's always fine, as long as the clerk likes wearing the earrings or other merchandise.

HIRING

Hire people who have (at least) an interest in the type of merchandise your store sells. Your best employees will have a *passion* for the kinds of items your store sells. That won't be every person who comes in with a résumé. Most people are not *suited* for retail because they don't naturally have the right disposition. What's needed is a disposition that is *intensely interested* and *positive*. I've heard that craigslist.com is a useful tool for hiring, but nothing will ever substitute for the actual energy of a person coming into your store with a résumé in hand. Even when you are not actively hiring, keep those résumés. A jewel (of an employee) could be hidden in there.

In hiring management, remember that a bright disposition is a must! A dour manager can sink your boat because you will have trouble keeping good employees. The attitude of management is a key factor in the type of chi energy that your store attracts. When I say "manager" I am referring to someone who is in charge of other employees. I am *not* referring to someone who is in charge of a department or a section in a store, but who doesn't boss other people.

Wisdom and experience are two qualities that a customer can immediately *sense* in a staff member. If you hire **age** (older people), you'll increase your chances of getting those two qualities *authentically* in the employee. You'll also have more reliability, because they will already know enough to *value* their job. Most older people have already figured out how to be nice to other people, so you won't have to *explain* that to your employee. More practice with *social skills* is what it boils down to. Video games have never honed anyone's social skills.

Hiring Smart! by Pierre Mornell is an excellent book about the hiring process. At the end of the book is a list of questions that you cannot legally ask without opening yourself to a lawsuit. *I Know What You're Thinking* by Lillian Glass is also useful to read before interviewing potential employees. It's a brilliant book about how to read people.

Firing is the other occasion when an employer is most vulnerable to lawsuits. When dismissing an employee keep it as yang as possible—say as little as is permitted by local laws and your own policies. "You are dismissed. Here is your final paycheck." The ex-employee is likely to cry and you will probably need to take a walk.

CUSTOMER INTERACTION

One of the greatest distinctions between internet stores and real bricks-and-mortar stores is the inevitable *customer and staff interaction* that takes place in a real store. Use that distinction to your advantage. Nothing is holding you back from proper employee training in **politeness**. Train your employees exactingly. Tell them to use certain exact words in certain situations.

In retail store work, you *must* train yourself to stay positive when dealing with customers. You are paid to *act* nice even if it doesn't come naturally in the situation. Each customer is a fresh new wave of energy, and the salesperson's job is to *surf* that wave the best they can. Stay buoyant and *attentive* throughout the interaction. If you were on a surfboard on a wave, you'd be *very* attentive. Customers can be annoying, but it's your job to *surf over* the tendency to be annoyed *with* them. A salesperson should never display annoyance or descend to their level and become mean or childish. The instant you do that is the same instant they feel truly *justified,* because you're obviously acting immaturely. You must retain poise and confidence even if you are turning the transaction over to someone who has *more* poise than you. The phrase from the restaurant world is "If you can't handle the customers, stay home." Poise can be defined by these words: ease, firmness, serenity, well-balanced, unprejudiced, mastery over self, having all your wits about you—all yang characteristics. Poise is *not*: labored or ponderous, stirred up or impetuous, irritated or timid.

There is only one way to handle customers—*individually*. Tune in one hundred percent to each customer you interact with every day, and look them in the eyes. Something in the customer *does notice* if you are fully paying attention to their words. It can be a bit exhausting, but you really have to do it in order for the transaction to sit right with the customer's psyche. At Green Apple Books I was called on to help with a customer service issue. A woman had phoned to see if we had a particular novel and was told that we had it in stock. Once she arrived, no one could find the book and the customer was *very* upset. She had good reason to be upset—she had driven, and parking is extremely difficult in that neighborhood. I looked for the book and confirmed that it was not on the shelf where it should be. I apologized for what had happened and said, "Since you like that author, have you read anything by John Fowles? I've noticed that readers of your author also like his books." I watched as all the tension drained out of her face. Someone *cared* that she got a good book to read. I didn't stop there—I love to match-make people and books. By the time she left, she was smiling and had purchased a stack of books a foot high.

When it's appropriate, bring the chi energy of your hand movement into use—you might physically *point* to the area of the store where the customer should go, in addition to describing it. When dealing with more than one customer, you can hold up an index finger when you *must* interrupt a customer. The one finger raised can be a subtle way of *asking permission* to interrupt. This example was mentioned in Chapter 3 under First Impressions.

Some people who come into your store aren't really customers—they are energy drains. They realize that a person behind a register is trapped and they see that as permission to talk endlessly, wasting your time or your employees' time. If that happens, recognize it immediately and disengage. Find something productive to do and busy yourself with it. Dust, clean, straighten, neaten, pick up the phone and tell someone their special order is in—basically stay *very* busy and don't pay attention to the person's rap. Go on with your busy life in retail and politely ignore them. If you give them the energy of your attention, you (or your employees) will be wasting time and running the risk of feeling drained when that person finally leaves. Your chi energy, and that of your employees, is valuable—it should remain vital. It is your way of staying in the moment and doing your job well. Retail is about work, and work requires energy.

Don't smile when delivering disappointing news to a customer. It's inappropriate and denies empathy with the customer. If you say, "No, I'm sorry we can't get that item for you" and you're smiling, the *impression* is that you are actually happy that you can't help them. You seem insincere, if not gloating. The customer isn't smiling when receiving bad news; empathize with them. *Continually put yourself in the customer's position.*

If you and a co-worker are talking about any customers, such a conversation *must* be held where there is *not even a slight possibility* that another customer could overhear you. If they were to hear you, your words would be throwing a bucket of water on their bright flaming *yang* enthusiasm for your store.

They could easily think: "Maybe they'll speak badly of *me* after I leave."

Never dampen your customer's enthusiasm for your store in any way. Please think on this principle as you pay attention to each customer. The customer should be a yang being—bright. Yin is dampening—so you and your employees have to also stay *bright* while at work. And without drugs! I feel sorry for any store where the owner is taking anti-depressant drugs. That situation is too yin and the owner needs to hire a manager who is not prone to depression.

During their work time, no employee (with the possible exception of managers) should ever talk or text on their cell phone or look at any portable electronic screen. If their phone is in their pocket and it vibrates, they should not look at it to see who called. Those things should be done only on their official break time and off the sales floor. You are paying for the employee's body *and mind*. The employee's attention should primarily be on the store and doing their job within it. If your cash register (or nearby computer) can also give your employees access to the internet, it should *only* be used for store purposes. If you have to discipline an employee about this, then you are not being forceful enough about it in the first place. Employees who cannot follow an instruction this basic are too immature to waste your time with. Earphones of any kind should never be worn by employees, unless they are required by management. (This kind of requirement is rare, or unheard of, in small, independent stores). A customer approaching an employee with an earphone on doesn't know whether or not the employee is listening to something important. The customer should have no reason for reluctance when approaching employees.

When a customer approaches you, try to match your response to their speed. If you notice someone coming toward you directly from the door, smile and look right at them. As they get closer, give the impression that you're ready to listen. Perhaps raise your eyebrows as a gesture saying, "How can I help?" They might say something like, "Where are dishes?" You should be ready with a quick, "Aisle two, on your left."

If, however, someone *ambles* up to your counter after they've been in the store for a while, and more leisurely asks where certain merchandise is located—be ready with a more *leisurely* response. Not to the point of being chatty—chattiness is yin, and should usually be avoided in retail. Use *a few* more words, and chose them well. Say something like, "Our small, but distinctive, dish department is over on aisle two. You'll see them on your left about half way down the aisle." You're being a little more leisurely in your response so that you don't jar their energy. Shopping is *therapy* for some customers, and it easy to startle a sensitive customer with a response that they might feel is too quick and abrupt.

Be sure to **smile** unless, as I said earlier, you have something disappointing to say, such as, "I'm sorry, we don't have pottery." Hopefully you know your neighbor stores well enough to say something like, "There's a very good pottery store a few blocks from here." **Any time you are physically directing a customer, always *point* with your hand and finger.** That motion of your hand and arm *moving* is a very yang act and helps to *propel* the customer to their destination.

CASHIERS

Cashiers should make every sale as speedily as possible. Don't delay people who are ready to give you money. We've all had the experience of being in line at a store while the cashier chats with a customer ahead of us after their particular transaction is over, or chats with another customer while ringing us up. Doing that makes us feel unvalued at that store. Cashiers can make or break a store. The line between loving and hating your store is a very narrow one for some customers—and often the cashier is the one who makes the difference. Don't allow an employee behind the cash register until you have trained and molded them into a polite representation of what your store is about. *Every* customer matters, even if you think you may never see them again. Even if there is no one else in line, make the sale speedily. The phone might ring, and you'll be ready to attend to it if your sales go quickly.

Cashiers should always *briefly* acknowledge the next customer in line while finishing up with the current customer. A smile and a look right in their eyes, perhaps with the words, "I'll be with you shortly" is *all it takes*. Be sure to acknowledge people if only with a smile. Never just ignore them until you've finished with your current transaction. The habit of doing that graciously is a sign of a very good cashier!

When giving change back to a customer, **always use your newest and flattest bills first**. Don't save them at the bottom of a stack of older bills. The first "spare-time" assignment for all cashiers is to neaten the bills in the cash drawer. Straighten any bent corners and put them all facing the same direction. It doesn't matter *which direction* the heads on the bills face, but they do need to all be facing the *same direction*. Any taped or badly torn bills should be placed at the bottom of their stack so that they go into a bank deposit rather than being used as change. If a customer hands you a wad of crumpled bills, straighten them enough to be sure that you are counting them correctly, but save your final straightening for after the customer has gone. Spending an undue amount of time straightening money that was just handed to you is a bit rude to the customer.

The best cashiers always count the change back to the

customer, putting *coins* into the customer's hand *first*. The customer can then close their hand around the coins and accept the bills with their thumb and forefinger. Putting coins on top of bills says you don't care if the customers' coins slip off the bills and slide away. It's insulting the customer at the very last moment.

It is a sign of an intelligent cashier to count the change back to the customer the old-fashioned way. They do the math in their head to count the change back to the customer properly. The smallest coins are counted back first and the largest bills are counted back last. This isn't for every store, especially during busy times, but it is distinctive and gracious. Graciousness usually does take a *bit* longer.

It's an extremely good idea to have your store's *return policy* printed on the receipt. It's easy to circumvent future bad feelings between your store and the customer by being clear about your return policy.

Always offer the customer the receipt for the sale. Not to offer the receipt is disrespectful to the customer. The receipt should be offered *after* it has been printed, so that the cashier has the receipt in their hand when offering it. Some customers would rather that you put the printed receipt into recycled paper because they know they won't need it. Other customers will be pleased that the receipt always comes with the sale. To the customer, a receipt that is offered by the cashier is a subtle clue that the business is **honest**. If no official ringing up of a sale happens, the customer wonders if the business is making sales but not recording them. Leave no room for suspicion as to the honestly of your business. If your store is useful in your customers' lives, they want you to stay in business. Honest businesses stay in business longer.

Always use BPA-free receipt paper in your cash registers.

Thermal cash register receipt paper is often coated with high levels of bisphenol-A, also known as BPA. This very harmful chemical is, among other things, an endocrine disruptor and is absorbed through the skin by those who handle the receipts. Cashiers press their fingers onto the receipts harder than customers do. They often have to tear them from the roll of receipt paper. Pregnant women are especially at risk. BPS (bisphenol-S) is being touted as a substitute for BPA, but research is indicating that it is at least as toxic as BPA.

Be grateful the customer came into your store in the first place. Be *very* grateful if they spent money. And then let them go on their way. Once you've smiled and said thank you, it's time to disengage. Don't just carry a conversation on and on. Find something else to do—help the next customer, straighten your cash register area—do *something* that needs attending to.

Never carry on a conversation with a third person when you are ringing up a customer—even if that person is your boss or coworker. Your boss should know better! Your attention should be on the person who is giving you money. Courtesy requires specific focus.

Cashiers should stand or have a high stool. Sitting in a standard-height chair is too yin and laidback for a cashier making sales. The customer could easily get the impression that the store is *just a hobby* for the owner. A standing cashier is ready to move and assist at a moment's notice. Provide something soft, such as a gel mat, for cashiers to stand on.

WORDS

Words are a powerful form of chi energy. It matters what *specific words* are used in dealing with customers. *Details* matter a lot in feng shui and in retail—exact words are important.

For the most part, your staff's first language should be the first language of a good percentage of your customers. The customers will subtly feel more at home in your store. *However,* a delightful accent in an employee's voice can create an instant positive impression for a customer. Good grammar, diction, and pronunciation are a must in all employees who deal with customers. Stores in multilingual neighborhoods should have some multilingual staff and signage. Then you are harvesting the chi energy in your own area.

There is no feng shui reason for your staff to introduce themselves to customers by first name. It can often seem pretentious. But in the right circumstances, such as sales that take more than one visit to complete, it can be helpful. Sales staff on commission will want to introduce themselves, and should have a store business card with their name on it to give the customers.

There is no need to say "sir" or "ma'am" to the customer. It can too easily come across as snobby.

If you find yourself saying, "What's up?" (most likely to your employees), use some other phrase. "What's up?" is too cutting and abrupt, and it's also quite unimaginative, implying that you are less than brilliant.

THE WORD "No"

Find some way to avoid saying the word "no" to a customer. In feng shui, it's a simple yin/yang issue. Yang is positive— yin is negative. Keep your store yang and positive. Instead of saying, "No, we're out of the item you want" to a customer—say something like: "I can check to see when it's due back in the store, and give you a call when it arrives." Put a **positive** twist on all customer interactions when it would be easy to just say "no." How you deliver negative news to a customer is the *essence* of the phrase "the customer is always right." The customer is sometimes very wrong about something, but you somehow avoid saying, "No, you're wrong." You may get a good laugh at some of the phrases you come up with, but those are not likely to be the best phrases to actually use. You may have to practice until you're good at putting a positive spin on bad news.

"The customer is always right" was drilled into me as a teenage cashier in a mall regional chain bookstore by manager Ruby Bratcher. Ruby was an *extremely* feisty woman and taught me with her every interaction with the customers. In 1970 a woman came to the mall dressed in what some people considered to be a see-through blouse. I heard about it when the manager of the shoe store next door came rushing over telling me there was a naked lady in his store and I should call the police. Ruby wasn't around to ask and I hadn't seen the woman, so I called the cops. Ruby was back in the store by the time the police officer arrived, and she just said to him, "Make sure nobody bothers her." I was extremely impressed by the *difference* in the two management styles. Ruby wasn't about to say, "**No**" to the customer, regardless of what she was wearing.

The final words of a transaction should never be "**No problem**." In fact that phrase shouldn't be used in retail *at all*. The problem with those particular words isn't just that they begin with the word "No," but that they indicate subtly that *the reason the help was given* was because it didn't inconvenience the *employee*. Yes, it's a subtle thing, but it's always there when those words are spoken. The last words to a customer should be, "You're welcome" which put the customer first. "You're welcome" is short for "You're welcome to my assistance" and it implies "You'll be welcome to my assistance *anytime* that I can help." The longer phrases are too wordy for retail, so stick with "You're welcome." It's best to be looking the customer in the eyes when saying it. You could also say. "Thank *you*, and have a good day (or evening)" or "Please come back to see us" or "My pleasure" or some grateful, cheery variant of those words—and of course, smile. That smile will already be on your face as you turn to help the next customer.

There are two occasions when "No problem" is an appropriate response to a customer. One is when a customer is actually *apologetic* about asking you for assistance. "Sorry to bother you, but I can't quite reach the item on the top row." The very best response is to say (while you are speedily getting the item down for the customer) is, "No problem. I'm *here* to help you." or "I'm happy to help." The other occasion to say "No problem" is when someone misdials and calls your store by accident. "No problem. We at such-and-such store stand ready to assist you if you need us" is a cheery response in the case of a misdial.

Frankly, the less you say the word "no" to a customer the better. Accentuate positive language and the customer will subtly have a nicer time in your store. *Never dwell on **any** negative subject with a customer.* The phrase "No worries" is also not good in retail—it starts with "No" and sounds too lackadaisical.

One of the rare times in retail when you must say "no" (or something very similar) is the instance of *unruly children.* Their energy is too chaotic for a retail environment. *Playground* energy is best reserved for the actual playground. It disturbs your merchandise and the other customers. Be as nice as you possibly can when asking the parents to control the children, but if the problem persists do not tolerate unruly children in your store. The root of the problem is the parents, who didn't raise their children properly, and if you lose *those* parents as customers, don't fret about it—go on to the next job at hand, which is likely to be a grateful customer.

The Telephone

Encourage employees to smile while talking to customers on the telephone (unless delivering bad news). The smile comes across loud and clear to the customer. In *Consult Yourself* Carol Harris says, "If you smile, it alters the shape of your vocal cords and your voice sounds warmer and friendlier." If the customer *hears* you smiling, it welcomes their chi energy in a positive way—from the beginning.

Answering in Person

Unless you are with a customer, answer the phone promptly. That's the proper *yang beginning* for welcoming the new fresh energy that is calling your store. The next thing you should do is also very *yang*—say the name of the store **and stop right there**. It's now the customer's turn to talk—let them do so ASAP.

Don't say, "How can I help you?" or "May I help you?" over the phone. Similar words are appropriate and gracious when spoken in the *physical presence* of the customer. But over the phone they're unnecessary and a waste of the customer's valuable time. They *called* in the first place because they wanted to *save* time. Otherwise they would have strolled in your door and asked you their question in person. Likewise, don't offer a greeting like "Good morning." With the proper lilt in your voice, you can say "Good morning" without having actually spoken the words.

The only time "How can I help you?" is appropriate *over the phone* is when it is spoken by a *manager* to whom the call is being referred by the person answering the phone. In that case, the manager should introduce themselves, state that they are a manager, and *then say,* "How can I help?" If the manager knows in advance that the call is a *complaint,* they should say something disarmingly gracious such as, "Thank you for taking the time to make this call. I'm Luanna—how can I set things right?" You've then done your best to prime the customer to be nice to you—hopefully they will be. Your wording has more or less said that you are on the customer's side. Your employees should know *when* a complex customer problem is best handled by a manager.

One of the big national chain bookstores (that recently declared bankruptcy) required its employees to quickly spout out a spiel about their current deal of the day before allowing the customer to say a word. (One of the problems with big box stores is the physical distance between upper management and the sales floor.) Any store that disrespects its customers so much as to waste their time with a spiel *first thing* over the phone *deserves* to go bankrupt. The *other* national chain bookstore still greets phone customers with a *recorded* advertisement, and I wonder how much longer they'll stay in business.

Don't answer the phone with something like "Thank you for calling such-and-such store." (Many chain stores do this, usually followed by, "How may I direct your call?") That's a waste of syllables, done for the sake of advertising their store's name. It's a waste of the caller's time and the customer is aware of this, and that's the *beginning* of irritating your customer. The "thank you" part of that phrase is always spoken too quickly and *never* feels authentic. Just answer the phone with the store name and *nothing more*—you've then quite graciously gotten out of the way. If your store is large enough to have a full-time operator, of course they need to immediately ask how to direct the call. Otherwise the *operator* gets asked questions that should be asked to the sales staff, and that's wasting the time of *two* people.

I recently called Walmart and the first thing I heard was

a recording: "Thank you for calling Walmart." That was immediately followed by an operator saying the exact same words. I felt as if I were being pounded.

How do you answer the telephone when your store has a one-syllable name? The name may be difficult for callers to understand, partly because *the process of answering the phone* can often be heard as well. It's best to add one or two more syllables. If the restaurant *Raw*, mentioned at the end of Chapter One (with a caution about the short name) had been a store, I would have recommended answering with something like "*Raw* food store." Add at least the word "store."

If you or an employee is in the store before or after hours and the phone rings, answer the phone in person. Not to do so is to deliberately cultivate the wrong attitude toward customers. Answer the customer's question, and at the very end of the call, tell the customer *gently* what the store hours are.

Even if you're answering the phone when the store is closed, don't answer with "Hello." If it's after hours, and your phone displays the number that is calling in, and it's someone you know and their call is expected, *then* it's fine to answer with "Hello" or "This is _____." Your name fills in the blank and answering that way is courteous, but not always necessary.

If your phone has Caller ID, don't answer the phone, "Hello, Mr. Brown." That's too abrupt and feels invasive. And there's always the chance that someone besides Mr. Brown is using his phone.

If an employee checks the shelf to see if an item is in stock, they should anticipate several other questions, and be ready with the answers, "Yes, we have three in stock. They're the quart-size and they're $15 each." That way the customer only has to then ask, "What time do you close?" When answering *that* question, say, "We close at 7 and open tomorrow at 9." Be sure to include the extra information about when the store opens. But don't say, "We're open 9 to 7" because that's an indirect way of answering the actual question. It indicates that the employee is not truly *listening* to the person who called.

Never rush a caller who has a complaint. Inexperienced employees should be carefully coached about the issue of when, and when not to, be *speedy* on the phone. Often for owners personally, handling these issues becomes second nature and they forget to instill proper responses into the employees.

If you, or any of your staff, ever answer the phone and the very first words that caller says are, "How are you?" or "How are you today?" disconnect the call immediately. To prolong such a nuisance call *slows* the yang nature of your business. *No one* calls a store (or any business) to ask how you are doing. The caller will be trying to sell you something shady that you don't need.

On Hold

During the time that a phone customer is on hold, you are almost saying "No" to them. Make every *on-hold* time as brief as possible. If the customer is on hold while you are checking on an item, dash quickly.

If a customer approaches you while you are on the phone you must decide whether the person on the phone would be upset by being asked to be put on hold. A person will not appreciate being put on hold when they have called about a problem. If another employee is available to help the customer in the store, alert them. Use your hand and finger to direct the customer to the other employee, or alert your coworker to the new customer by using a bell or hand signal.

If you're the only employee in the store and you're on the phone and a customer walks up to you—look at the customers' eyes and smile while holding up an index finger. Your finger is saying, "Please wait one moment." As soon as possible ask the phone customer to be put on hold.

Before putting a phone customer on hold, it's best to say "May I put you on hold?" and then *wait* for a yes from the person on the phone. You may not get a yes, in which case you need to be ready to quickly offer, before they have to suggest it, that you can call them right back. And then be sure to call them back *as soon as possible*. If you're in an *extreme hurry* you can say to the person the phone, "Hold, please." but you *must* include the "please." This phrase should only be used in rare instances, because of its abruptness.

When a customer is put on hold, they should not have to listen to advertisements or music. That's not why they called your store. Silence is fine. Silence makes it plain to the customer when a live voice from your store finally says, "Thanks for waiting—how can I help?" After a customer has been put on hold, it's *definitely fine* to go ahead and say, "How can I help." You don't even need the word "you" at the end—the customer knows who you are talking to. Get on with helping them. Don't delay by even one word.

Call your store and ask to be put on hold. If there are one or two loud beeps, get a different system for putting callers on hold. As a customer patiently waits on the phone, don't tax their goodwill by putting beeps in their ear. Beeps when you're on hold are puzzling and thereby quite yin.

Answering Machine

For your store to have its maximum success **there must be an answering machine on** when the store is not open and there's no one to answer in person. Otherwise, you are not harvesting all the chi energy that is *trying* to come your way.

Without an answering machine the store's message to some of its potential customers is "Don't bother calling, because we're not answering." The least thing an answering machine can do is to inform the caller of the store's hours. The *best* thing an answering machine can do is to *accept* messages from the caller.

Your answering machine should pick up after one or two rings. If it is possible to call your store and after many rings get the message, "Please enter your remote assess code," you need to change that. Customer hearing those words have been given them a huge invitation to *never* call your store again.

The **voice** on your answering machine is often the *first thing* that greets a new potential customer. The person recording that message should be slightly smiling when speaking your store's message. The person should sound cheerful and energetic. Here's where an accent with an *authentic* lilt is perfect because of its delightfulness. Two of my own favorite lilts are Irish and Caribbean.

Chapter 4   Money Changing Hands

Ka-ching! Money changing hands is the essence of retail. The right **product** sells to the customer at the right **price**. This extremely yang act is what all retail is built upon. It's an agreeable exchange with *money flowing in your direction*. The person (you or your employee) who buys from vendors is in a key position. The judgment of the buyer as to product and price is crucial in making ka-ching happen.

The Price

There are quite a few pricing methods used in retail, with some stores using more than one method. Some methods are more yang (better for retail) than others, but it is possible to be too yang. When a pricing method is very yin it is *usually* best to avoid it.

Stores in which every item in the store is the same price (or almost the same price) are *too* yang. This system is too limiting and never recommended. A few stores, selling cheap-quality plastic items, use this pricing strategy.

The next most yang pricing system is one in which every item is priced at a dollar amount, such as $4.00, $25.00, $100.00. Looked at from a feng shui view, it has a large dose of yang quickness, tempered with a multitude of price points to add interest. This is a bold choice for a store, but boldness is appropriate in retail. Customers perceive this method as being honest.

This next advice is for those stores that are prosperous enough to afford it. Absorbing sales tax is a very yang way to do business. It can allow you to round your prices and have the final bill to the customer be in a round number. You may not even need coins in your cash register. That will speed up cash drawer counting.

Price lining is the term for having a specific number of prices for a category of merchandise—in the shirt department, the prices could be $10, $25, and $60. It's yang because it's simple—three choices (in this example). Price lining is appropriate only for certain stores, and certain types of merchandise. This method also has the advantage of simplifying merchandise comparison.

Odd pricing is extremely common in retail. It's the name for having prices end in 5, 8, or 9. Odd pricing is inferior from a feng shui point of view, because it is excessively yin. The prices are difficult to add up in your head, and the pricer is hoping the customer will think the merchandise is more of a bargain than it really is. Customers subtly perceive this as *less than honest*.

Having prices that end in increments of 25 cents is far superior to odd pricing. And counting your cash drawer will definitely be quicker.

Multi-unit pricing—fifty cents each or three items for a dollar— works well in certain situations in certain stores. The per-unit item is more expensive than the same item in the multi-unit *deal*. This pricing method has a marvelous mix of yin and yang—it's complicated, but not *too* complicated. And the result can be nicely yang—more items sold!

Private label brand pricing is very advantageous for regional chain stores, and any store that has regional chain aspirations. Your store brand is cheaper than other brands you sell—it's a very yang strategy because it adds power to the name of your store. Go for it—if it's *appropriate* for your store. Don't, however, allow your private label to result in a diminished selection on your shelves. If your brand looks like a monopoly within your store, your shelves can easily start to seem monotonous.

Keeping your prices non-negotiable is advised for all stores— it's the simple yang way to do business. The obvious exceptions to that are second-hand stores, including antique stores. Even most second-hand bookstores don't allow price negotiation. If your store is not a second-hand store, keep your prices firm, and have any exceptions posted plainly and proudly—such as senior discounts. My first bookstore offered a ten percent discount to anyone shopping on the day of the full moon.

A discount offered on certain days or to certain people (such as seniors) is a type of flexible pricing. This pricing method is only as yang as it is uncomplicated. Ace Hardware offers seniors a discount *if* the purchase is made on a certain day of the week. Customer loyalty plays a big part in how complicated you can get with this pricing method.

Bundle pricing is a mix of yin and yang and it works well in certain stores and in certain seasons. Gift stores often have gift baskets already put together with one price for the whole thing—the bundle. The yin aspect of bundle pricing is that there are *many items*. The yang aspect is that there is only *one price*. If your store has had good experience with this method of pricing then continue.

There are occasions when the wholesaler may tell you, the retailer, what price to charge. You just say, "Yes" and do it honorably. To do otherwise would introduce a yin element because you would be duplicitous. That's not simple, nor is it advised.

The price often determines whether an item sells. If certain product isn't selling at all, you must mark it down (or return it if that's an option). Creating movement where there was stillness may involve having a markdown sale on that item and then not carrying it again. If it's an item that you intend to *always keep in stock* no matter how slowly it sells, then you must charge what is necessary to stay in business.

Rare and one-of-a-kind items in specialized stores can take a while to sell, but in the meantime, your store has gotten the reputation for having unusual things (if that's what your store sells). Your store may also get a reputation for charging a lot of money. I've heard of a rare book dealer making a unique response to the question by a customer, "Is this book really worth this much?" His response was, "Not yet." That's an extremely intelligent response. It takes a *confident* pricer to say something like that, one who *knows* how rare an item is. The response is yang, verging on being too yang. It's a response that most stores dare not utter.

Whatever price you charge, accept these five ways of payment:

- Cash
- Check
- Debit card
- Mastercard
- Visa

Accept other forms of credit card payment if you feel you need to, but remember: simpler is better.

A varied price point makes a very appealing store. Some things are so affordable that a child can buy them with coins, and some things are so expensive that most customers can't afford them—*most* customers, but not all.

Your price sticker on merchandise should never hide the ingredients list or the place of origin of the product.

THE PRODUCT

The product mix is what's actually for sale in your store—the mix of merchandise. Think carefully about what you throw into the mix. Coming from a background in bookselling, I was appalled to discover the big box bookstore chains had cafes within the bookstore proper. When I realized that a customer could take an expensive photography book, go over to the café, and eat their greasy food while browsing the book, I realized, "This business doesn't value the products they are selling. These books are just commodities that they can return to the publisher or distributor. Lots of books are *for sale* in here, but it's not a real bookstore." Real bookstores are owned and run by people who love books. It's well known that when books and food mix, the books suffer.

Once the products have changed hands the items usually need to go into a bag. If a customer provides their own packages say, "Thank you" and help pack the items. The packaging you provide for your merchandise *represents your store*. It's advantageous to have the name of your store on the bag, especially if there is also the color red. I recommend providing paper bags instead of plastic, unless it is raining. The thin slick plastic bags that most stores give away *feel too insubstantial* to be an emblem of strength, support, and dependability. Use plastic bags in rainy weather, but give away durable paper bags otherwise. The *sound* of paper bags is more natural than the sound of rustling plastic bags. In some stores the option of a reused bag is a possibility. While it *is* more ecological to use, it is also a bit more difficult to put your store name on a reused bag.

Advice to Buyers

The buyer is the person in your store who does the buying from vendors and sales reps. Often it's the owner, and rightly so—*new stock buying* is one of the most enjoyable tasks in retail. Ordering new stock is quite different from the routine buying of items that are regularly stocked. Not everyone gets the enjoyment of seeing products that aren't already in stores in your area. Buyers of new products are in a key position in culture. Routine buying should be turned over to employees who are interested in the products a particular vendor sells. If an owner turns over *new stock buying* to employees, those people must already be very experienced buyers *within your store*.

Stay curious about the type of product you carry. *Never* be hesitant to add another vendor. If your store feels distinctive and nice, the word *competition* is less likely to be in your vocabulary, and your attitude is more likely to be "There's no such thing as competition for our store—we're unique." Think of your store as a wonderful place, and continue to create and improve that. I once offered to give a store owner a wholesale catalog of great merchandise at great prices only to hear, "We don't want to add *one* more vendor." Too bad—the mix suffers and the store is more ordinary and less recommended. I continue to hear people bemoaning what a great store it *could be*—but it's not.

When Crown Books opened one of their national chain stores three blocks from Green Apple Books, the owner of Green Apple did only one thing differently—he marked all the *New*

York Times bestseller books down to thirty percent off, the same as Crown. The Crown store was tiny, the staff was poorly paid and therefore unknowledgeable about books, and the store had nothing unique going for it. Green Apple basically stomped their butts. Crown closed, and no one missed them. If a competing store opens near you, the proper response is derisive laughter. *Let them* bring more shoppers into the neighborhood—the more the merrier!

The direction of your merchandise mix is going to be geared toward the future *or not*, based on how sustainable the resources are that went into making the merchandise in your store. *Reuse is the economy of the future*—J. I. Rodale said that. The only retailing I still do is to voluntarily manage the gift shop at our church. I confess to obtaining *part* of the merchandise mix via eBay where shopping is worldwide for vintage and new items. The result is quite charming in a very small space.

Selling products that people really *need* is the most sure-fire way to avoid going under in economic bad times. Selling things that are interesting or beautiful but not terribly *useful* gets much tougher in slow economic times.

I sincerely hope you don't just order a bunch of disposable plastic items. Those things need to be avoided for the life of the Earth. A *huge* amount of plastic is floating in all the world's oceans, mostly in very tiny particles. We should reduce plastic production in the first place, for the sake of the planet—feng shui won't do a heck of a lot of good on an ecologically wrecked planet. The roots of feng shui are in *nature*—and that's the end of my plea for less plastic.

Another way that a buyer can help the chi energy of the planet is to order products that are made in the same country as your store. Less energy is wasted in transportation, and a huge percentage of customers *do notice* and respond positively, especially older customers who understand deeply that this also helps their local economy. Stores that spotlight products made in their own country are experiencing large boosts in sales, often double-digit increases!

Chapter 5   Visual Presentation

A good product mix is what puts a smile on their face, but what puts the *sparkle* in their eyes is the *way the product is presented*. **Merchandise** (rhymes with dice) is the items you sell; **merchandize** (rhymes with dies) is how you sell them—how the items are presented or displayed. The two words are usually spelled the same, but they are almost always pronounced differently. I spell them differently here, to differentiate them. Merchandise sells better if it's merchandized well. Sometimes it's as easy as shuffling things around—mixing the mix. The essence of the art of retail is to make your store look *interesting*—retail entertainment!

Signage

The larger the store, the more important it is to have signs. But even small stores benefit from some signage, so that shy customers don't have to ask common questions.

Departments & Categories

Very small stores don't usually need departmental signs, which are always large. However, category signs have an important place in most stores. They quickly clarify for the customer what type of merchandise is in a section. This is especially important in stores where one type of item (mystery novels in a bookstore, for example) is extremely similar to another type of item (such as true crime books). Clarity is yang and very desirable in retail.

Point-of-Sale

A point-of-sale sign is a card placed with an item on a shelf that gives the customer more information about the item. These signs can be in a sign holder or just attached to the shelf, depending on the image you want for your store. Some point-of-sale signs bring attention to sale items, and these signs are usually on colored paper or have a colored border around them. *Shelf talkers* are another kind of point-of-sale signage that do the talking when a clerk is busy. They explain why the item is unique and worthy of purchase. Shelf talkers should be used with discretion and *only* for items that are truly special. Never use more that two per unit of shelving. Everything can't be special, and overusing shelf talkers will cause customers to ignore them.

Shelf labels, in general, need to be at least as large as the edge of the shelf. They can be a bit bigger, but they should not be any smaller. If they do not reach from the top of the edge of the shelf to the bottom of the edge, they will frequently be overlooked. The edge of a shelf is *a long straight line* and the eye tends to follow straight lines quickly. If you want to *catch the eye*, you must do a thorough job of *interrupting* that line.

DISPLAYS

Your displays either make sales or they don't make sales, based on how the merchandise *looks* to people. A person who is skilled at visual merchandizing knows the principles of attracting the eye just as well as the artist who paints on canvas. Draw the eye and delight the mind. Grab their attention and don't let go!

In any art there are amateurs and there are experts. Never let an inexperienced employee set up your displays or do visual merchandizing. Your store is not a place for anyone to *practice*. It takes an experienced eye to place an object where it is most expressive. You can learn the art by informing yourself of the principles, and through practice. Any display needs *neatening* after a while, however, and *anyone* on the sales staff should neaten a mess when they notice it. It is their constant job (when they aren't busy doing something else) to make the store look nicer and neater.

DESIGN

Some people are naturally better at design than others, but with practice and education anyone can improve greatly. Search for visual merchandising books on Amazon, note the books that interest you, then order them on interlibrary loan. You will learn, and it will be fun and inexpensive. Good visual displays use the **five principles of design:**

Balance is an essential feng shui principle and it's also the number one principle of design. The balance can be formal (symmetrical), with one side being the mirror image of the other side, or informal (asymmetrical). When using informal balance, divide the display in half, left and right, then compare the visual importance of the two sides. More visual weight should usually be on the left side, since our eyes often focus there first—as if we were reading the display like a page. Having strong colors and heavy objects near the *bottom* of the display will assure balance in an up and down direction. The bottom should never seem lighter than the top, or the display will feel wrong. Formal balance is more dignified, and informal balance is more active; the goods to be displayed should be a deciding factor in which type of balance to use. A pleasing equilibrium should be discernable in the display.

Harmony goes hand-in-hand with balance. It's something I always stress in my consultations. Harmony is *agreement* and without it there is chaos. Chaos may draw the eye, but it also draws a frown. And few people continue to look at a chaotic display; it's ugly and never looks correct. The elements of harmony are size, shape, and texture. Harmony requires *one idea* per display.

Lines and their repetition bring harmony. Don't accentuate more than two different *kinds* of lines per display. There are four kinds of lines, and they are all equally useful, because display is about *products*, and products vary *infinitely*. Yang lines are best for yang, masculine merchandise, and yin lines best for feminine.

- Vertical lines are the most yang. They move the eye up and down and add the illusion of height.
- Diagonal lines are also quite yang. A line from the upper left to the lower right is often used because the eye follows it quickly, naturally, and actively. Such a line also adds a look of stability to a display.
- Curved lines *excel* at moving the eye. They are a bit yin, but perfect in the appropriate display.
- Horizontal lines go from side to side in a display. They

are the most restful, yin lines. The eye just glides along. Mattresses are horizontal for good reason.

Proportion is your best way to never have something look *off* in your displays. Space division is required as your display accumulates merchandise and props. Those items relate to each other and divide the space. There are four arrangements for dividing the display space:

- *Pyramid* arrangements are formal and extremely common.
- *Step* arrangements are less formal and are most effective when there are three steps.
- *Zigzag* arrangements require precision in order not to look chaotic.
- *Repetition* is the simplest kind of arrangement, but it can be boring. A bit of change creates interest.

Rhythm brings beauty. Fine architecture has been described as frozen music. When you set up your displays you are creating architecture on a small scale. Our eyes are curious and they eagerly follow a path. There should be *visual motion* once the eye has first noticed the display—this conveys vitality. Guide the eye throughout the display so that all the different items of merchandise are noticed. *Repeating a shape* is like repeating a note of music, and it is the simplest way to create rhythm in a display. A swinging, continuous line is a very graceful way to make rhythm. Draped fabric is commonly used to create such a line. Also, if you consistently increase or decrease the size of *objects of a similar shape* a rhythm is created. The most formal way to create rhythm is by using a mandala or sunburst design, like wheel spokes that radiate from the visual center of the display. This rhythm-creating method works best when there is a strong visual frame around the display, otherwise the eye could easily follow the line of a spoke and leave the display too quickly.

Emphasis is what *first* grabs the eye in a display. For best visual coverage, start the eye slightly above the center or in the upper left corner. Emphasis is created by using *motion* or objects that are *large* or *contrasting*. The contrast can come from shape, color, or texture.

Beyond these five design principles, you have no set rules in your displays—except to continue to surprise people!

DISPLAY AREAS

If your shopping area allows you to have sidewalk sales displays, then *have them*! If people walking or riding by see other people in front of your store browsing, they're going to be attracted. Something in them is going to be curious. "Why are those people browsing? What are they looking at? Maybe there are some really great deals there."

Avoid bare glass edges in your display shelving. They symbolize severe cutting energy in feng shui. Among the worst offenders in this category of display fixtures are glass cubes held together with metal fasteners. There are a lot of bare edges on those cubes, and it would be best to use a different type of fixture. Clear plastic shelving and display units are not a problem. Plastic may *look* like glass, but it is a very different material.

If you have display shelving with bare glass edges and would like to keep using it, cover the edges that face out toward the customer. Use strips of wood, bamboo, metal, plastic, or rubber. An L-shaped flexible molding that works well for most glass edges is available from brandsport.com. This molding is manufactured for the edges of car doors. See Sources.

Ceilings are a neglected display space in most stores. You're paying as much rent on the ceiling as you are on the floor. Hang things that are for sale (not just signage) from your ceiling if you possibly can. Break out of the envelope a bit, and be creative with display. Someone once walked into one of my stores and quickly came to a stop. He said, "I just want to stand here and look. There's so much to see." *Mesmerize your customers.* Enchant them with delightful merchandise in displays that draw them in. *Some stores* should utilize almost every square inch of available space. Selling from the ceiling has the advantage of causing your customers to *look up.* That's an optimistic gesture; even the phrase is optimistic. And looking up is considered in feng shui to be *lifting* chi energy—both yang and positive.

MERCHANDISE & PROPS

Every object that is for sale in a display needs a bit of space around it—room for its aura. If objects are too crowded together, it becomes difficult to see them individually and the customer's eye is tempted to move along without lingering. This doesn't apply to a cluster of *items that are all the same*, such as a pyramid of food cans.

Sell more of what's selling. As soon as you notice sales picking up on an item, begin spotlighting it. Do so in whatever way is appropriate in the situation—maybe move it to eye-level, or display it near the register, or first thing when you come into the store.

If you are unsure which department an item will sell best in, feel free to try the item in more than one department. If it sells well in both departments, keep it in both departments.

When considering props for use in displays, remember

this: **Never have items on display that could be mistaken for merchandise.** If a customer ever hears the words "Oh, *that's* not for sale" they will instantly hate your store. They may not show that in their words and actions, but they won't come back and they'll never recommend you. When they asked the price, they had already imagined the joy of owning the object—and you just ripped that joy to pieces. This is often a problem with display furniture in antique stores. I've been in some stores with high ceilings where the space above the shelving is used to display artwork that is not for sale. I can't recommend that because it's too yin and museum-like for a store. If you have *anything* on the sales floor that looks like it could possibly be for sale, but is *not* for sale, put a sign on it saying **Not for Sale**. Tiny change—*huge* improvement! This is even better advice: put a price on it, so high that if someone really paid that, you wouldn't mind parting with it—you could replace it or get something as good. Make the customer happy, and they'll make you happy.

Seasonal displays and decorations *can* get out of hand, especially near the end of the year. People come to your store to *buy merchandise*, not to be amazed by how much decoration you can cram into one store. Don't let exuberant decor compete with the goods. It doesn't take much to put seasonal cheer into a store, and *restraint* is the better part of valor when it comes to seasonal decor. Display windows are the best place for eye-catching decor. I remember one store that filled their front window with a Troll nativity scene at Christmas. It was designed by the Troll manufacturers, and every person and animal in the scene had fuzzy Troll hair, wide open arms, and a huge grin. It was impossible to see it and *not* smile.

Maintenance is part of display, and it invites *fresh* chi energy into the store. There should be no areas-that-don't-look-good visible to the customer. Items on the sales floor should be dusted *almost* every day. A high-quality feather duster is ideal, but they're not cheap (and they don't have artificially-colored feathers). When the floor is cleaned don't use a broom, which stirs up more dust. Use a canister vacuum cleaner, which *removes* the dust. A dusty store *never* reaches its potential—clean it. The best janitor is someone who knows how to *look for dirt*, not just clean robotically. Pay special attention to the cash register area from the customer's point of view.

DISPLAY MIRRORS

Displaying merchandise on a horizontal mirrored surface symbolically *doubles* the merchandise. Choose merchandise that looks sensible and pleasing when reflected.

A very important feng shui rule is: **Do not have mirrors directly facing each other**—not on the sales floor and not in dressing rooms. If a customer needs see their back, use mirrors with hinges. When no one is using the dressing mirror, adjust the side mirrors so they do not directly face each other. See Fig 5.1.

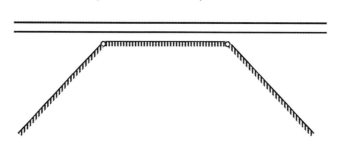

These mirrors are on hinges and are adjusted so no mirror directly faces another mirror.

Fig. 5.1

Direct-facing mirrors are often found at the ends of refrigerated produce display units. A solution is to cover one of the mirrors with frosted plastic contact paper. When I notice direct-facing mirrors in homes, I often hear from the resident about hauntings or other unpleasant occurrences near the mirrors. No direct-facing mirrors—not at your store and not in your home!

A plinth is an object that raises the height of merchandise in a display. They are sometimes called cubes. Don't use large *mirrored* cubes, because the side mirrors *chop up* a person's reflection. This reflection-chopping is a *severe* problem in a home, but even in stores it should be avoided except for very small plinths that hold items like precious jewelry.

ENDCAPS

If your store has aisles, it should have endcaps—they are a world in themselves! Cap off *all* rows of shelving with endcaps. Rounded endcaps are best, but anything is better than seeing the side of the shelving unit at the end of a row next to an aisle. Endcaps represent an incredible opportunity to sell merchandise at the end of a row.

If you have plain wooden shelving and that's all the aisle space allows, use tiny hooks or pushpins and hang light, thin merchandise on the sides of shelves. If the shelves are metal, use magnetic hooks. Sell the magnets if they're appropriate as merchandise in your store. (It's difficult for me to recommend refrigerator magnets *too* much—because I usually tell my household clients to eliminate most, if not all, of them from their refrigerators. They easily amount to clutter in a home.)

At least half your endcaps should have merchandise at *regular* prices. The other half of your endcaps can have sale items—a mixture of both advertised sale items *and* unadvertised sale items. The former items may have brought people into your store, but the latter items keep your customers *alert*. The non-sale endcaps are for seasonal displays or impulse items.

SPINNING RACKS

Spinning racks are a great invention. They are excellent for the chi energy of stores.

- They *suggest* movement, even when they are still.
- When they *do* move, it's customer's *hands* moving them. Causing a customer to touch your display is very good news for sales—someone's hand is almost touching your product. *Touching* the product is ninety percent of getting it to the register.
- They suggest *joy* and *glee*. Spinning racks combine the element of *surprise* with physical *proximity*—and the result is better sales.
- They're space efficient—at least they *should* be. The best spinning racks have somewhat complicated designs creating an amazing amount of *pockets* or spaces to display merchandise.

WINDOWS

Try to change your window displays *at least* once a month. If those displays don't stagnate, it's likely that the merchandise on your shelves won't stagnate either.

As with any display, a window display should be well lit and have one main message or idea. The public passing by your window isn't going to take the time to figure out what the message of the window is. They give you precious little time to make that message abundantly clear. Be bold and simple, and remember: The overriding concern is always to sell merchandise.

Moving objects are very powerful attention-getters in windows. However, don't use moving *lights* in a display unless your store *sells* those lights.

Chapter 6   Layout

Cash Wrap Areas

Allow the customer to find the cashier easily. That's the first rule of cash register placement. If possible, allow the cashiers to have an *empowered view*—a wide view of the sales floor. Their view should include the *entrance into the store* if possible. No customer should be able to see into the cash drawer of your register; that would be empowering the *customer* too much.

In smaller stores the cashier is often the only employee in the store. If this is the case, be quite careful in positioning the cash wrap counter. Allow the cashier to see both the entrance *and* the sales floor. It can be tricky to do this, especially if there are important display windows. It's never good for a passerby to be able to look through your store window and see the back of the cashier or the area on the employee side of the counter.

The top surface of the cash wrap counter can be almost any material that stays looking good with heavy use. The exception is stone which is too cold and harsh. Metal is also quite cold and is best reserved for sales of food items, where it conveys the impression of heightened sanitation. Glass countertops are fine as long as the bare edge of the glass does not extend beyond the surface that supports it.

If the cash wrap counter is L-shaped it can cause a type of subtle harsh energy called a poison arrow. The counter's sharp right angle aims a specific straight line outward into the room, as in Fig. 6.1. There are two places where a poison arrow should *not* aim: at the front door, or at the office. If a poison arrow *is* aimed at either of those places:

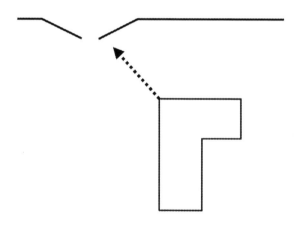

Cash wrap counter points at front door. Not good!

Fig. 6.1

- *Reposition* the counter so the arrow misses the door or office, as in Fig. 6.2.

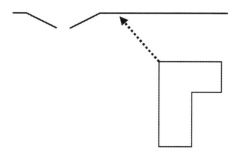

Corner of counter does not aim at the door. Much better!

Fig. 6.2

- *Round* the sharp corner, from countertop to floor level. Fig. 6.3 shows a rounded counter. Rounded vertical corners are *always preferred* for retail because they are streamlined and allow for swift, safe passage. Customers perceive rounded counters as friendly and approachable. If the curve is unique and gracious, customers are tempted to move their hands along it—a great place for impulse items.

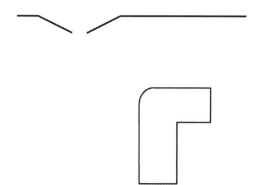

This rounded corner does not make a poison arrow.

Fig. 6.3

- Put a *spinning rack* on the floor at the point of the corner, as in Fig. 6.4.

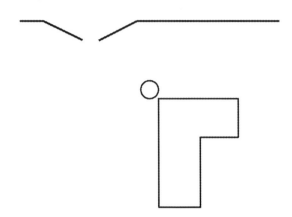

A revolving display rack at the sharp corner creates friendlier energy.

Fig. 6.4

SALES FLOOR

Whatever you do (or *have* to do, depending on your circumstances) keep your sales floor plainly laid out and uncomplicated, *but* without having all long, straight aisles. Break up those aisles a bit, just not in a *confusing* way. Let the customer know exactly where they are at all times. Getting lost in a store doesn't feel good, and if you're shopping in a hurry it feels *horrible*. Keep it yang and simple, with a bit of meander on your longest aisles. A *meander* is very different from a *pinch*. A pinch is a constriction of chi energy, where customers going in one direction have to wait for customers going in the other direction to pass. The *waiting* is yin and it should be avoided in retail.

If the front door of the store is in a direct line with a back door, the symbolic meaning is that prosperity may leave too quickly. The best way to correct this is to place a free-standing display somewhere in that direct line between the two doors. If you can't *see* the back door from the front door, all is well—energy is going to your merchandise rather than leaving the store.

Shape of sales floor

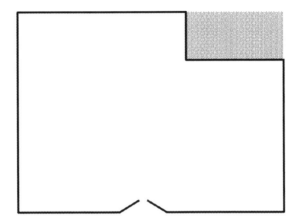

The shaded area is *missing* from the sales floor.

Fig. 6.5

According to feng shui an ideal sales floor should be a square or a rectangle, which most sales floors are. But some sales floors have an L-shape, often caused by the location of the office. Even a slight L-shape suggests that *something is missing*—maybe customers, maybe money to pay bills, maybe the right employees. To correct this situation a symbolic cure is needed. Place mirrors as shown in Figure 6.6.

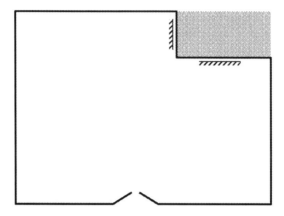

The two mirrors face into the store. They symbolically
bring back the missing area.

Fig. 6.6

The shiny side of the mirror should face into the store, and the
bigger the mirror the better. What you are trying to create is a
feeling that your store is larger than it is, and a very large mirror
can do that. If a large mirror won't work in your situation, use
any size that will work—you can even use a dime-size mirror.
The mirror can be quite visible or it can be totally obscured by
other objects such as merchandise. If a mirror shows the lovely
back side of some nice merchandise, even better—in feng shui
terms you are increasing the value of your store because you
are seeing the merchandise twice. But remember, *never* put two
mirrors directly facing each other on the sales floor or in any
room, as shown in Figure 6.7. The energy that is created by two
directly-facing mirrors is *extremely* inauspicious.

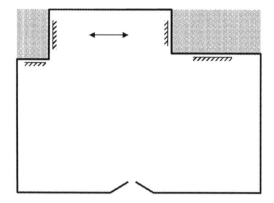

There are two mirrors that directly face each other. Don't
ever do that!

Fig. 6.7

When placing the mirror to symbolically increase the size of
your store, say out loud that your intention is to make the sales
floor be a perfect square or rectangle, with nothing missing. Say
something like: "I am placing this mirror to symbolize that the
room is bigger and has a regular shape."

Floor level changes

If possible, *avoid floor level changes* on the sales floor. They
are another subtle way of repelling vital chi energy. The older
a customer is, the less they appreciate floor level changes. And
(*generally* speaking) the older a customer is the more money
they have accumulated. Value these customers; don't discourage
them.

If small floor level changes cannot be avoided, *change the
color or material of the floor where the change occurs.* Let the color
or material change indicate one thing only—floor level change.
Customers' eyes should be able to stay on the merchandise
without concern about tripping or stumbling. Unless your store
sells floor coverings (displayed on the floor) you shouldn't be

drawing their eyes downward. This is not an advantageous direction to pull chi energy.

Free-standing support poles

Large stores often have free-standing poles to support the weight of the roof or upper floor. These poles can signify argument because the symbolism is: one eye sees on one side of the pole and one eye sees on the other side. We see things differently. The pole is a visual *divider*.

If at all possible, incorporate such poles into display shelving so they are not noticed at eye level. If that's not possible, put mirrors on one or all sides of the pole, assuming it is a square pole. The mirrors may be large and cut to fit the sides of the pole exactly or they may be very small and discreetly placed. If the pole is round, a very small mirror will do. When placing the mirror say, "This mirror symbolizes that the pole has been erased. No arguments in this store." or words to that effect.

BULLETIN BOARDS & EVENT POSTERS

It is not a feng shui concern whether or not a store has a community bulletin board. But if it *does* have one, or allows fliers for events to be posted, it is a huge feng shui concern *where* that bulletin board goes: *It must be in the back of the store.* The chi energy that comes into your store *must* go past merchandise before reaching an area of event postings or bulletin boards. This does not apply to notices about events taking place in your own store. In that case, **do not be subtle**. Splash it all over your store, inside and out, to the degree that is appropriate for your store. Not all stores have an employee bulletin board, but if your store does, common sense decrees that it should be visible only to you and your staff.

No flier should be posted in your windows (or on your glass

door) if that event is not taking place in your store. If you make *even one exception* you will be hurting the feelings of everyone who has ever been turned down in the past, so you cannot make one single exception ever. Your windows allow a person to gaze into your store, and when a flier is posted the person reading it is being told that they can get what they want (information about an upcoming event) without bothering to come into the same room as your merchandise. You must lure them inside, and then past as much merchandise as possible. The existence of your store is a community service, and allowing the posting of fliers and notices is a huge community service—which your store could not offer if it went out of business. Profit and community service can and *should* go hand-in-hand.

No political signs should be posted in your windows, other than one that simply says "Vote!" If you post a political sign, you are undoubtedly alienating *some* of your customers. Electoral neutrality is best for stores because all money is equal. If you want to put up political signs, do so at your home. If there is a local initiative on your ballot that directly impacts stores in your area, it is fine to alert the public to your position on that initiative. Do not espouse political views loudly while on the sales floor.

TOILET LOCATION

If there is a shared toilet that is quite separate from your actual store you are fortunate, because there are many potential problems that come along with the convenience of having toilets on the same premises as the sales floor.

The biggest concerns are about the drains and the *relation of the drains* to the **office** and the **cash registers**. Water represents money in feng shui and drains are places where water *leaves*. The drains symbolize your wealth and good fortune draining away. It is best to have the places where money is handled (cash registers and offices) at some distance away from drains—especially from the toilet, which has the largest drain hole. Any toilet in your store should have an actual *lid* on it, not just a seat. To encourage employees (and the public, if it's a public toilet) to close the lid, get the type of lid that gently closes itself with just a slight nudge downward. They're called *soft close* because they can't slam.

It's not good to have a toilet near to the **entrance** of the store, because that symbolizes fresh opportunities (represented by the entrance) being flushed away before they bring benefit to the business.

If a toilet or other drain is near the *three important areas*—cash register, entrance, and office desk—put a mirror, with the shiny side facing the drain, somewhere between the affected area and the drain. Figure 6.8 shows the placement of a tiny mirror placed behind the toilet tank, so it is not seen.

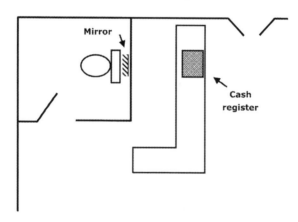

The small mirror is placed on the wall behind the toilet tank, and shines toward the toilet.

Fig. 6.8

- Put a mirror on the wall between the drain and any of

three important areas. If the mirror is in the room with the drain (usually a bathroom) the shiny side faces into the room. If this mirror can be seen by anyone who might think it is a camera, then put the mirror on the *other side* of the bathroom wall, as shown in Fig. 6.9. It will then be in the same room as one of the three important areas. Face the shiny side to the *wall*, because on the other side of the wall is the drain. You can paint over the back of the mirror so it isn't noticeable.

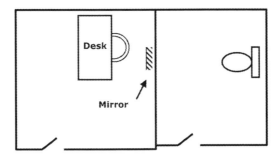

The mirror is on the office wall, and the shiny side faces
toward the toilet in the next room.

Fig. 6.9

- Less commonly, a toilet (or other drain) is directly *above* one of the three important areas. You'll need to put a small mirror on the ceiling with the shiny side facing the ceiling. Place the mirror as exactly as you can, with your goal being to place it directly under the toilet drain.
- If it's a *sink* that's above one of the three important areas, you could alternatively place the mirror directly under the sink in the upstairs room. The shiny side faces up toward the sink.
- Sometimes the drain is *below* one of the three important

areas. In this case the mirror should be placed on the ceiling of the room with the drain. The shiny side faces down toward the drain.

In all the above instances, be sure to *say out loud* that your purpose is to symbolically reflect away the influence of the drain on the prosperity of your business. Any time the shiny side of a mirror is facing a wall, it's fine to paint over the back so the mirror is less obvious. You could even caulk around the edges for a finer look.

The restroom door must be kept closed when someone is not coming or going. If the office door and the restroom door are directly across from each other hang a clear, disco-ball shaped, faceted crystal somewhere in a direct line between the two doors. Say out loud something like: "This is to symbolize the dispersion of the drain energy before it reaches the office."

CHAPTER 7   OFFICES

Blessed are they who have separate rooms for offices. Many small stores don't have a separate office room, and that's too bad. The separate room gives you plenty of opportunities to do **office** feng shui, which is quite different from the feng shui of the public parts of your business.

There are many books on feng shui for the office, and two are in Recommended Reading. Most have some valuable information, however almost all of them discuss your lucky direction in relation to positioning your desk. That is Compass School Feng Shui, which is not the kind I practice. I'm a Landform School practitioner. In Landform School Feng Shui the *form of the room* is what furniture placement is based on.

The door is the mouth of the room and you want to be able to see it when you are spending significant time in the room. **Be able to see the office entry door easily from the desk.** If the desk must be placed so that your back is to the door, use a convex mirror or silver glass ball. Locate the mirror or ball so when you are doing deskwork you can easily see behind you.

Have a solid wall behind you when you are sitting at your desk. The wall represents strength, solidity, and backing. A window behind your back symbolizes an abyss—no support. Extra support is gained by hanging *a picture of a mountain* on the wall behind your back. There should not be a body of water in the foreground and the mountain in the background. Such a picture doesn't convey as much *strength* as a simple mountain picture.

What about office and desk clutter? Slick, minimalist offices are rare in retail for good reason. Life is just too busy to keep a retail office picture-perfect at all times. It boils down to individual visual temperament. Some people function well with a light dusting of clutter, and other people are bothered by it. The desk I typed this book on would be considered rather cluttered by some people, my partner included. But I can find everything I'm looking for in moments, and nothing gets lost. Albert Einstein said, "If a cluttered desk is a sign of a cluttered mind, of what, then, is an empty desk a sign?"

Locate the office at the rear of the store if you can. Don't limit the valuable sales floor space at the front of the store. More people come into the front of the store than will go all the way to the back. Also, office personnel are less likely to be bothered with trivial matters if they are toward the rear. If the office *must* be toward the front of the store, make it a *small* office.

Do not have a *home* office as the *main* office for your store because the home is too yin. Don't use a home-office tax deduction because it can trigger an audit. When necessary bring home a package of things that you need to work on, but then take it back to the store before too long.

The office can be any gentle color that makes you feel good. Yellow is excellent, as well as sage green. I'll reiterate the importance of removing bits of old stuck tape anywhere in the office. If there are pin holes in the walls—spackle them. The holes may be small, but they still represent energy leaking away.

Your desk chair should be comfortable and provide support for your back and elbows. The lumbar region of your spine should have a correct lordosis—curving forward toward your stomach. It should feel natural to be upright; slouching should feel wrong. I recommend *Treat Your Own Back* by Robin McKenzie. The exercises are well illustrated and will help you stand tall.

No matter how comfortable your desk chair is, it's killing you if you use it too frequently. Sitting more than six hours a day makes people forty percent more likely to die within fifteen years, as compared to people who sit less than three. That's even with exercise as part of a person's routine, according to a study on sedentary time reported in *Diabetologia* (2012). If you can, do some of your office work while standing.

When writing emails, always *reread* them before clicking the SEND button.

ELECTROMAGNETIC FIELDS

The dangers of electromagnetic fields were stressed in Chapter 2. EMFs can be elevated in offices because of certain electrical equipment. Flat-screen computer monitors with separate keypads are best. The old-fashioned computer screens that bulged in the back were quite bad for people. Sit at least five feet away from that kind of screen. If you are closer, you are being exposed to very high EMFs aimed at your vital organs from a cathode ray gun. The only reason you don't die outright is that there is so much lead in those *glass screens* that the government asks that we dispose of the screens as toxic waste.

Computer manufacturers are no longer using the word *laptop* because the first four inches above and below most laptops have very strong EMFs. If you set it in your lap (when it's turned on) you're zapping your lower organs. If you type on it you're zapping the bones of your fingers. Some of the newer devices such as iPads have no EMFs. Separate keypads have no EMFs, even the wireless ones.

Other sources of EMFs in offices:

- **Portable wireless telephones** can have very strong EMFs, depending on the manufacturer. We have switched from a V-Tech to a Panasonic for that reason. Any telephone *receiver* that has a cord connected to the wall has no EMFs, and is preferred.
- Many **adding machines** have very strong EMFs for the first few inches above them, right where you fingers are. However, some electric adding machines (such as Activa) have almost no EMFs; that's much better for your fingers.
- **Electric staplers** can have *extremely* elevated EMFs that extend as much as four feet from the device even when it is turned off. They need to be unplugged when not in use.
- **Breaker boxes** have strong EMFs extending one to four feet around them. Measure with a gaussmeter if your desk is close to a breaker box.
- **Big batteries** cause dangerously strong EMFs for quite a large distance around them. Ten feet is not unusual for some very large batteries, such as the one I tested in a large hardware store. It caused the next-door office to have unsafe EMFs *throughout the room*. If you have a large backup battery in your office area, test the EMFs.

CHAPTER 8   RETAIL DETAILS

ADVERTISING

"Early to bed, early to rise. Work like hell and advertise." That was the motto of Dr. Scholl, the footwear manufacturer. Some established retail stores scarcely need to advertise in order to stay in business. But staying in business and *prospering* are two different things. Every retail store needs *some* form of advertising even if it's just fliers posted on bulletin boards. Never post a notice about your store in an illegal location, such as an electric power pole. Your store would then be associated with *breaking the law*.

Multifaceted advertising is best. People need to *see the name of your store* three times for it to stick in their memory.

Not every business needs to be listed in the Yellow Pages, but every *retail store* does need to be listed. Have at least a line listing in the Yellow Pages of the *real* phone company in your area. Do not waste money buying a listing in any Yellow Pages that does not come from the real phone company. Have good internet presence on sites like Yelp and Facebook, but don't count on all your customers finding you through the internet.

Every store should have **business cards**. Bookstores should have free promotional bookmarks, as well as business cards. The cards should be standard size and they should look balanced, top and bottom and side to side. The balance does not have to be formal and symmetrical; it can be a pleasantly asymmetrical balance. The cards should definitely not look jarring or chaotic. If you're at a loss for ideas, look through one or two editions of *The Best of Business Card Design* from Rockport Publishers. Evelyn Lip has written the best feng shui book for business design, *Design & Feng Shui: Logos, Trademarks & Signboards.* It's the first book in Recommended Reading. If a whole book on the subject is more than you care to know, there are six succinct pages on logo design in Jes Lim's *Feng Shui for Business & Office,* which is also in Recommended Reading.

On promotional material such as business cards, **use a fat, bold font for the name of the store.** *Never* have a very skinny font for the name of your store. Bold says you've got **plenty** (and can *accept* plenty). A more slender font can be used for any of the other information on the card. But the *name* is special—it *is* the business that it represents when viewed by the reader.

Your store's *telephone number* is the main thing a customer needs from a business card. It should stand out and be quite noticeable. You will then be drawing more chi energy into your store. Stores often make the mistake of printing their fax number directly below (or next to) their phone number, and in the same size font. In feng shui terms, this is confusing to chi energy. It's very easy to juxtapose the numbers and misdial when calling. The same thing can happen if the address number is located very close to the phone number. This was mentioned in Chapter

2, but it bears repeating—if you have a phone number that spells words, also write the numbers out (i.e. 867-0431).

Some *red* color on the card makes it more noticeable, but don't overdo it, and don't use red lettering unless it is outlined in black. Store business cards should not have a predominately black background. That would be too yin. It's good to have your store hours printed on your business card. If the hours are complicated, use the back of the card.

If you haven't opened your store yet and don't have an email address for it, pick one that will be easy for your employees to say quickly to someone over the phone without a substantial chance of being misheard by the caller. Avoid using the domain name of your internet service provider, because if you change providers you will be forced to change your email address. Never change your email address. You won't know about it, but you will forever loose *some* contacts.

INTERNET

This book is about the *experience* of being in a bricks-and-mortar store. An internet store is much more about *information* than it is about *experience*. But all retail stores (larger than a shoebox) should have a web presence. It's best to keep that internet presence from greatly affecting the sales floor when the store is open. If you need to be looking at a computer screen for much of the day, your back should not be toward the door or sales floor. Greeting chi energy with your back turned is a cold welcome. Customers should see *your face* even if you are looking at a computer screen. That being said, here are some tips for your website:

- Make it *readable*. One company's homepage had red letters on a red background. They said they got feedback that it was difficult to read, but they were going to keep it that way because they thought it was good feng shui. (They had been given this advice by a feng shui consultant). Yes, red is frequently used in feng shui, but in this context it was silly.

- Make your site *simple*, without animation or flashy things that will cause the pages to load slowly. Especially do not have animation or movement of any kind on your homepage. Merriam-Webster.com is a great example of what *not* to do—it's much too busy.

  Your site can be as simple as one page with your store name, address, phone number and hours. Also there should be at least two pictures of your store, one inside and one outside. I use a Pinterest link on the homepage of my site fungshway.com. It easily and freely allows me to post new pictures of feng shui-friendly products. People can get to my Pinterest pictures without having to *join* Pinterest—which gives Pinterest an advantage over Facebook for *certain* uses.

- Make it easy to *contact* you. The customer should have the choice of emailing or calling.

- Have a good, easy to find (and easy to use) *search* function on your site. Many sites use Google Search within their site. It's not as good as a carefully detailed search designed for your site.

- The customers should be in *control* as much as possible. Let them decide how many items are displayed on a page.

- There's a website that critiques other websites, called websitesthatsuck.com. Seeing what *not* to do is a powerful learning experience.

If items are sold through your website, look for these features in your e-commerce vendor:

- Your site must be *secure* and the customer must have no doubt about it. Use very trusted companies such as Verisign or Paypal to give confidence to shoppers.
- Make your site speedy to navigate and always let the customer know exactly where they are in the purchasing process.
- Allow the customer to make a *wish list* on your site.
- Allow them to freely edit their cart.
- Sell more of what's selling. If a customer buys something (or puts it on their wish list) let them know what else other customers who bought that item also bought.

OWNERSHIP

Yang is best in retail and the most yang type of ownership is individual ownership, because decisions can be made swiftly when there's one person in charge. General partnership is the next most yang form of ownership and it is also desirable. Corporations are the most yin type of ownership because they are more complicated. Small, privately owned corporations where the stock is held by one person or just a few people (who are actively involved in management) are also a good option for stores.

The type of corporate ownership that is *not preferred* is the large publicly owned corporation because the owners (stockholders) are too far removed from the actual sales floor. These businesses are often run for the benefit of the stockholders, not for the customers in the store. Sears has become an example of this. They have had stores in prime locations, but they are currently selling those stores for their real estate value. This obviously has no benefit for their customers, but a huge benefit for the stockholders.

Starting a business is easier than running one successfully. Keeping it going is the hard part. And the *really* hard part is letting go of your business—selling it. This is when you'll be glad you didn't name your store something personal like Gloria's Gifts. Having an emotional attachment to owning something is detrimental to selling it, and that includes a store. Once you've decided to sell the store, you have also taken on the job of improving the look of the store *constantly* until it sells. Perfection in every way is your goal.

SECURITY

All the good feng shui in the world won't stop shoplifters if your store is an easy mark. Don't let it be! Use locked display cases for *liftable* items, and if necessary use large convex mirrors to see obscure areas of your store. Cameras and electronic security systems are often appropriate in large stores. None of these will offend your *real* customers—they *want* you to stay in business.

I remember Mary's Thrift Store in downtown Huntsville, Alabama in the late 1960's had a sign saying "Shoplifting is between you and the Lord." That is always ultimately the case, but Mary's little store didn't last very long. *Take shoplifting seriously* and train your staff to be on the alert for it. If an employee notices even slightly suspicious behavior, they should immediately alert at least one other employee. "The Lord helps those stores who help themselves," I say.

Also, your store must be secure from break-ins—this is a *basic* feng shui concern. Use *locks* and use them every time. Armed robbery is a rare thing for retail stores, but train your staff not to argue with a gun.

RETAIL IS DETAIL

One small detail is the orientation of the grooves in the screw heads of the switchplate and wall-socket screws. The grooves should be vertical, which is a yang direction. At home the grooves can be vertical or horizontal, but in the store set them all vertical.

If any (non-merchandise) thing in your store is broken and cannot be immediately fixed, put a red dot on it and say out loud, "You are fixed. You are no longer broken." The red dot can be very small and put in a discreet place. Some people use the red dots that are sold in office supply stores and other people use red nail polish. The symbol of the red in this case is *new blood—fresh situation*. If *safety* is an issue in a broken item, fix it immediately.

SHOPPING BASKETS

If your store offers hand-held baskets for use while shopping, good for you—you will have increased sales. The very *presence* of the baskets says, "You will need this—there's *so much* to buy here!" The most important consideration in selecting basket style is *hand comfort*. Wire handles are too skinny and press into the fingers that are holding them. Plastic handles are usually fine. They can be a problem if there are two handles and holding them is clumsy. My favorite baskets are the old-fashioned metal and canvas kind that have a handle with rounded wood beneath the metal. They are comfortable, distinctive, and environmentally-friendly.

LUCKY CAT FIGURINES

Some stores have lucky cat figurines on display. The owners are hoping the maneki-neko (their Japanese name) with one paw up will beckon prosperity to their stores. It won't—a figurine can't do that. It's superstition to believe it can. The only stores that should have them on display are stores that sell them. Otherwise someone may ask, "How much does that cost?" And you'll have to say, "Oh, we don't sell that. You'll have to go to *some other store* to buy that."

ACCOUNTING & TAXES

Protecting truth is important and always will be. If you are not being honest in any way in your business accounting, change that immediately. Otherwise you are likely to attract *other* dishonest people into your store and your life. Keeping track of falsehoods and duplicities is a misuse of your brain—it overcomplicates the busy-ness in your mind, and does not serve the yang purpose of your store.

Pay your taxes. Keep only one true record of your business. The record of your business is **your business talking to you**. Your business will be telling you lies if you don't keep honest records. Don't even think of keeping *two sets of records*, one real and one fake. The message you'll be sending out will be "What can be trusted?" and somehow the Universe will cause you to feel that you can't trust people—your employees or your customers or both. You'll worry more if you don't keep honest records. If you do keep honest records you'll sleep better and probably live longer. This brings us to the next topic: how the feng shui of your home influences the success of your business.

Chapter 9   You & Your Home

The chi energy of the owner, as well as of any managers, is a great factor in the long-term success of a store. I've seen businesses make it through hard times by the sheer willpower of the owner. If the owner burns out, the business will suffer. You *must* be a well-rested boss. When you are around your employees, you must *not* swear, use inappropriate humor, or be sexist, racist, arrogant, disrespectful, or rude. You must be good at keeping confidential information. If you need ideas and inspiration to change your personal habits, read *Life's Greatest Lessons: 20 Things That Matter* by Hal Urban.

Stay fit, even if it means exercising in your office. Once when I worked at Green Apple Books I had a meeting with Rich Savoy, the owner and founder of the store. In the middle of my report, he got down on the floor and started doing pushups. As I continued with my report and recommendations, I understood how he maintained his fitness and stamina. I've since found out that pushups, even wall pushups, are a particularly good exercise to keep the brain sharp.

Working in retail and being around customers all day can leave you feeling drained. One of the best ways to wash the workday away when you come home is to bathe. Take a quick shower if that's all you have time for, but if it's been a particularly demanding day, take a hot bath with sea salt added to the water. Your energy will be greatly restored.

Don't assume that only extroverts (who are more yang) are suited to own or work in retail stores. I'm an introvert (more yin) but when my *role* is to be an owner or manager and to deal with the public on the sales floor, I jump into it with gusto. However, introverts get exhausted by that role. We *must* have quiet time afterwards to recuperate. Your spirit can be restored by solitude and nature. If your life has balance, you'll last longer. I recommend *Quiet: The Power of Introverts in a World That Can't Stop Talking* by Susan Cain.

The way that you should *not* relax after a workday is by sitting in an electric massage chair. I call them *electric chairs*. The electromagnetic fields are incredibly powerful and *all* of your vital organs are getting zapped. Some of those chairs must be *unplugged* before they are safe to sit in.

No one likes to receive business calls on their private line, but for a store owner it's sometimes unavoidable. When someone calls your home land line or cell phone and needs to leave a message, it must be clear that they have reached *your* phone. The message on your answering machine should be in your voice and say your name. Do not use a generic message that simply tells the caller what number they have dialed.

It's important to know that feng shui is always *only a piece of the whole picture*. Other factors affecting your business success are: your education (and its continuation), your discernment, your judgment, who your friends are, and how you've treated people.

YOUR HOME

For the owner, *the shape of your house* also matters greatly for the success of your business because your business and your life are interrelated. In your own home, you are sending a message out to the Universe as to whether you want things to go well or not. That message is being broadcast by the objects that you own—their shape, color, symbolism, and where they are placed. Your home is where **the bagua** comes into play, giving individual significance to the corners, sides, and center of the space. Some consultants say the bagua matters for the sales floor of your store, but in my experience that is not the case because no one *lives* in your store.

In the following checklist are the feng shui home problems that I consider to be most important for store owners. The first six items apply to a freestanding house or a unit such as a condo or apartment. The last four apply primarily to a freestanding house.

- Is a bathroom in the center of the house? See **Center Bathroom**, below.
- Is a bathroom in the far left corner of your home? See **Wealth Corner Bathroom.**
- Is there a central spiral staircase? See **Central Spiral Staircase.**
- Is the bedroom doorway hard to see as you lie in bed? See **Empowered Position for Bed.**
- Is either of the two back corners of the home *missing*? See **Missing Back Corners.**
- Are there interior upward stairs in a direct line with the front door, visible from just inside the front door? See **Stairs in Line With Front Door.**

- Does the landscape slope steeply down behind the house? See **Steep Downward Slope Behind Home.**
- Is the lot triangular? See **Triangular Lot.**
- Is there a tree directly in front of the front door? See **Tree in Line With Front Door.**
- Are your outside front stairs open, without risers? See **Risers on Front Stairs.**

Center Bathroom

The location of the bathroom, more than that of any other room, can make or break a house. The most important thing is this: Don't have a bathroom in the center! This means that you *shouldn't have a bathroom that is totally enclosed within a house.* It must touch an outside wall. See Fig. 9.1.

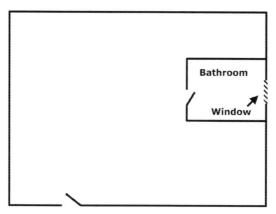

A healthy bathroom has at least one side tangent to an outside wall, preferably with a window.

Fig. 9.1

If you live in an apartment, the outside wall is just the perimeter of your apartment. If you can walk in rooms of your house all around the bathroom, it counts as being in the center. Do not ever buy a house like this! Throughout the history of humanity, toilets have usually been outbuildings. It is only recently that they have been located under the same roof as the living space. To bring them into the *core* of that space just doesn't work energetically! I have known the histories of some of those buildings—bankruptcy, divorce, disease, and so forth.

If you already live in a home with a totally enclosed toilet, I urge you to relocate the bathroom, or move. If that is impossible, here's a list of some things you can do to help the situation:

- Put a bagua mirror outside the bathroom above the door. This is one of the rare instances when I believe it is okay to put a bagua mirror inside the home; some consultants discourage any indoor use of a bagua mirror.
- Use metallic paint or wallpaper on the walls inside the bathroom. This symbolically *seals* the room from the rest of the home. See Sources for examples of quality metallic paint and wallpaper.
- If there is more than one bathroom in the house, do not use the center one. Guests may use it. If there is a skylight, grow lots of plants so that it seems like a greenhouse.
- Keep the door closed (as with any bathroom), and preferably mirrored on the outside.
- Hang a tiny wind chime just inside the bathroom door. Just as the door opens about four inches, the top of the door should slightly touch the bottom extension of the chime.

WEALTH CORNER BATHROOM

The two back corners of a home are often referred to as the power corners. The Wealth or Fortunate Blessings area of the home is the *back left corner*, as you stand at the front door looking into the home. See Fig. 9.3.

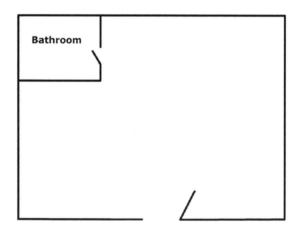

Wealth Corner Bathroom
in the far left corner of the home.

Fig. 9.3

It is not good to have a bathroom in the Fortunate Blessings area of the house or apartment. The symbolism is that your good fortune is draining away. In this case, however, there *is* a lot you can do to change the dynamic:

- The toilet lid should always be down when the toilet is not in use. It is important to have the lid already down when you push the handle to flush. I recommend the lids that gently close themselves with the slight touch of a finger.
- The door should always be closed, and preferably mirrored on the outside. Hardware stores sell small, inexpensive hinge-pin closers. They are easy to install, and will automatically shut the door.
- Put one or two large rounded stones at the rear base of your toilet. Glue felt to their bottoms if there's any chance of damage to floor tiles. The stones act as a grounding medium. They're large. They're solid. They couldn't possibly get flushed. They're gonna stay there!
Instead of stones, you could use 25-pound flat barbell weights. These are also appropriate to place in the cabinet under the bathroom sink, where they ground your good fortune before it drains away.
- The plant Sansevieria (Snake Plant or Mother-in-Law's Tongue) can be used effectively around the toilet to counter the *flush* vibration. Its strong uprising form very effectively says "no" to that down-and-out vibration. Place it in pots on the floor on each side of the toilet tank. Snug the pots right up against the wall, and as far under the tank as they can go without bending the leaves. If your tank is out from the wall a bit, you might even have leaves coming up from behind the tank. Of course don't have any of the leaves terribly close to the seat. A pot of Sansevieria can also be placed on top of the toilet tank if the tank has a flat top.

- Affix a small mirror to the bathroom ceiling directly over the toilet seat, reflecting down onto the toilet. Double-sided tape works well to hold the mirror. Say out loud, "This is to confine the energy of the toilet."

CENTRAL SPIRAL STAIRCASE

This problem is not common in homes, I'm glad to say. Spiral stairs in the center of the house represent a corkscrew through the heart. Stairs are considered spiral if they curve around enough so that some steps are directly above other steps. They're cute, but they can easily cause a slight disorientation that creates a major problem in feng shui. Hang a crystal or wind chime from the ceiling over the stairs and say, "This is to disperse the energy of the stairs so they don't affect the rest of the home." Also, if possible, have an upward-shaped plant somewhere near the base of the stairs to symbolically lift energy.

EMPOWERED POSITION FOR BED

The more time you spend in a particular place or room, the more resonance it has in your life, and on an average people spend a third of their lives in their bed. Your bed is therefore the most important object in your home. There are rules upon rules when it comes to placing a bed. Being able to see the doorway is just one of them. When you can see the doorway (without moving your head more than ninety degrees) you are in an empowered position, sometimes called a command position. When you can't see the doorway, you've disempowered yourself and are set up for surprises that you may be unprepared for. Things will seem to come out of *left field*.

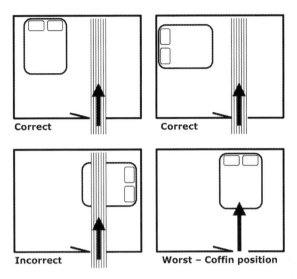

Bed position relative to chi from the door.

Fig. 9.4

Others rules for bed placement are:

- Don't place the bed so that the head is on a wall with a toilet on the other side. If this must happen, place a small mirror on the wall between the bed and the toilet with the reflective side facing the toilet—symbolically reflecting it away. The mirror can be in the bedroom or the bathroom. If it is in the bedroom the reflective side faces the wall. If the mirror is in the bathroom put it behind the toilet tank with the shiny side toward the toilet. Say out loud that the mirror symbolizes your wish that the *toilet drain energy* not affect your bedroom.
- Don't place your bed (especially your head) right next to a window, unless the window is several feet above the bed.
- Don't place a bed directly in line with the door. If you have no alternative, hang a clear crystal between the

door and the bed. Hang it above head-level so you don't bump into it. Say out loud something like: "This crystal is to disperse any harsh energy from the doorway before it reaches the bed."

- Dead bodies are traditionally removed from a room feet first. If you sleep with your feet pointed directly out the bedroom door you're in the *coffin position*, and your full body is in the pathway of the swath of strong energy from the door. Fig. 9.5 shows the coffin position and what is *not* a coffin position, where the bed is not in line with the door.

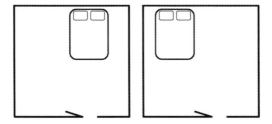

The bed on the left is in the coffin position. The bed on the right is not in the coffin position, and it is fine.

Fig. 9.5

- Do not sleep under an open beam. If there is no alternative, hang a clear, disco-ball shaped crystal from the bottom of the beam and say out loud, "This is to disperse any harsh energy from the beam before it reaches the bed."
- If a couple sleeps in the bed, it is important that one person does not have to crawl over the other to get out of bed. Try to have at least eighteen inches on either side of the bed for walking around. Allow at least eighteen inches *anywhere* you expect people to pass by; otherwise you are pinching chi energy.

When all these rules are applied, it sometimes leaves only one obvious place for the bed. But sometimes there is *no* ideal place for the bed, in which case a mirror may be needed so that the door is easily visible. A freestanding dressing mirror is often ideal. Locate the mirror so you easily see the door as you lie in bed. Some feng shui teachers like bedroom mirrors, and others caution against them, but all agree that it's fine to use a mirror to see the door.

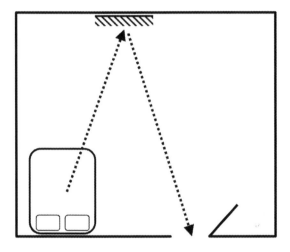

The mirror is positioned to show the door.

Fig. 9.6

MISSING BACK CORNERS

A perfect square or rectangle is considered to be the ideal shape for a floor plan. Any deviation from that should be thought of as either an extension or a missing area. Extensions (such as bay windows) are generally to your benefit, but missing areas can be a big problem.

The bagua is a diagram used in feng shui for interior spaces. You can think of it as a big yin/yang symbol that lies over the floor plan of the home. The entrance door is at the yin part of the yin/yang. The bagua grid is further divided into nine areas, and these areas relate to aspects of a person's life.

Of most concern in retail are the two most yang corners of the bagua. The far left corner is the Wealth Corner and the far right corner is the Relationship Corner. If either of those areas is missing because the back wall indents into the house's ideal rectangular shape, you have a great disadvantage. No Wealth Corner could signify less money, and no Relationship Corner could signify fewer customers or problematic employees. Remodeling your home to build out those corners is the *real* solution, but since that's seldom feasible, mirrors are used as a symbolic solution.

This solution is exactly the same as in Chapter 6, Shape of the Sales Floor. A mirror (the larger the better) placed on an inside wall of the missing area, facing the living space, is an effective solution. The mirror symbolically enlarges the home just as a decorator uses large mirrors to make a small room seem larger. When placing the mirror say, "This enlarges the home so there is no missing area," or words to that effect.

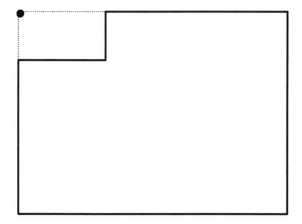

The point marks the apex of the missing area.

Fig. 9.7

A second solution, if you have access to the missing space, is to symbolically claim it. Note where point A is in Fig. 9.7. It is the apex of whichever area is missing. Try to keep that apex (point A) quite accessible. If possible, do something attention-getting at that point. Frequently used items are:

- An outdoor pole lamp
- A fountain or sculpture
- A birdbath or birdfeeder
- A clothesline

By placing something very noticeable at the apex, you are giving that missing area some much-needed spatial definition.

If the apex of a missing area is in the bottom of a swimming pool, use waterproof glue to affix one or more coins there. In the Wealth Corner one coin is enough but it should be costly and face up. In the Relationship Corner, two coins should be used and they should face each other, as if they were talking.

A woman attended one of my classes in Hawaii where I mentioned it was good to keep a fountain going in the Wealth Corner of the home. She and her husband owned a coffee shop. He laughed at the idea, but she did it anyway. They had set a goal for their business of a certain amount of money they would like to make in one day. They had never reached that goal and didn't expect to until the next Ironman Triathalon, which was months away. That same week they reached the goal and two days later they surpassed it. She thought she'd have some fun with him and said, "You know, I think you're right. That fountain had nothing to do with reaching the goal. I'm going to put it away." He said, "Oh, no, you don't!" One of my favorite things in feng shui is to see skeptics turn around because of good results.

If you do put a fountain in your home Wealth Corner: it should not have a light below the water (which says conflict) and it must be kept going, otherwise it says *dried up*. The fountain may be turned off when you are sleeping or away from home, but otherwise it *must* be kept flowing.

STAIRS IN LINE WITH FRONT DOOR

If stairs to the upper floor are directly in front of (and facing) the entrance door, the chi may not stay inside your house. Imagine the chi bounding into your house, heading directly up the stairs, losing momentum, then rolling back down, and out your front door. That's pretty much what happens. It is less likely to happen if the stairs are more than 12 feet from the door. In that case, the chi has plenty of time to slow down on the lower floor and begin to circulate there. Stairs that are less than 12 feet from (and directly facing) the front door would benefit from having a large potted plant at the bottom. The plant form should be uprising, not drooping. A very large floor vase or umbrella stand could also work, symbolically catching the chi that is trying to leave. Putting a bagua mirror inside above the door is also recommended.

STEEP DOWNWARD SLOPE BEHIND HOME

If the land drops off dramatically behind your house (as is the case in many homes with sweeping views) put a moving weathervane on top of your house to lift the energy upward. If you can add exterior lighting, do so with uplights that shine upward onto the back of the building. Also, if it is possible, add a fountain outside your front door, with the water flowing toward the front door area or flowing 360 degrees, like an umbrella. This solution is subtle, but powerful. If the fountain flows constantly, it will continually oppose the dynamic set up by the lay of the land. In fact, it is *always* a good idea to have a water feature (a small pond or gentle fountain) in your front yard. It reinforces the feeling that the front yard is lower than the back yard, as if water were flowing down to collect in your front yard.

TRIANGULAR LOT

Feng shui prefers regularly shaped lots—four sides in either a square or a rectangle—for a balanced life. Any lot with a bizarrely shaped map outline is not advisable. Triangular lots are the most extreme, having only three sides. The message is that something important is likely to be missing in your life. The worst triangular shape is one with a tight acute angle. See Fig. 9.8. The worst scenario is that the front door faces directly toward a tight, narrow corner of the lot. It suggests that things could get tighter for you in the future.

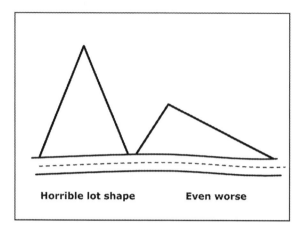

Horrible lot shape   **Even worse**

Triangular lots

Fig. 9.8

This lot-shape advice is for a residence. If the property will be used *only* commercially, a bad lot shape is not likely to be a severe problem. The busy yang nature of commercial use can overcome it.

Lights, mirrors, and good landscaping are your choices as solutions for a triangular home lot:

- Fill in the tight corners of the lot with plantings that give the impression that the lot shape is squarer.
- Put mirrors at the edge of your property, near the corners, facing into your property. They symbolically expand the property. The mirrors can be small, and they should face in toward your property. You can put them on small metal stakes, such as hardware stores sell for holding reflectors.
- Try to light up any tight corners on your lot. It symbolically expands them. An electric light on a pole is the usual recommendation, but it can sometimes look

awkward. Solar lights are good, as are the little lights on a string. Any light is better than no light. The light needs to function and be used at least occasionally.

- If outdoor lighting seems like a waste of electricity, *let nature make light for you.* Plants with white variegation on the leaves make an area feel lighter and therefore more open. On moonlit nights the area *glows* very noticeably. Ask a nursery or landscape consultant which white variegated plants will do well in your climate. Variegated plants are available in all sizes from low ground covers to mighty trees.

- If the front door is facing a tight corner, put a mirror outside the front door, facing away from the house. A bagua mirror would be best. The mirror pushes the tight energy away from the home.

TREE IN LINE WITH FRONT DOOR

A large object such as a tree or electric pole, in a direct line between the street and your front door, represents an obstacle. I'm a great lover of trees but right outside your door is not the right place for one. If the obstruction is not removable, there are two symbolic solutions: A small bagua mirror can be hung above your front door. If you don't like the look of a bagua mirror, then any mirror or very shiny, reflective, object (such as a brass doorknocker) will do. Another symbolic solution is to change the *purpose* of the *obstacle.* It can become a *holder of an affirmation.* To do that, you just put a real physical affirmation up in the tree. It could be a recovery coin that had a positive saying on it, or a small rock with "love" or "peace" carved on it, or just a piece of metal foil that you emboss with words such as "look up, be well."

RISERS ON FRONT STAIRS

If there are stairs going up to your front door they should have risers as well as treads. See Fig. 9.9. Stairs going up to back doors and side doors don't have to have risers. It's good for interior stairs to have risers, but it's not vital. Risers are the vertical parts of stairs that connect the treads. When you walk upstairs they are the part that your toes are pointing towards. They are rarely a structural necessity but energetically they are vital. If you can see right through the stairs, the chi energy is doing exactly what your eyes are doing. It is slipping through the open spaces and moving on, not rising up to your living space where it's needed.

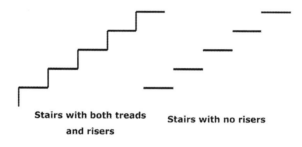

Stairs with both treads and risers   **Stairs with no risers**

Stairs with and without risers

Fig. 9.9

One client could not add risers because she was a renter. Instead she stapled beautiful red oilcloth where the risers would have been. It was stunning and quickly effective in her life.

There are certain kinds of cement stairs that resist any kind of riser addition. In that case, you are missing a *huge percent* of the chi energy that would otherwise be coming to you. Moving is usually not an option, so do everything in your power to bring the *visual energy* up the stairs. An exterior fountain or wind chime near your front door would be good. Also, do everything you can to visually emphasize your door. You probably can't overdo it because the situation is quite serious and calls for a *standout* front door. Just be sure not to over-clutter the area.

If a condominium or apartment building has no risers on its stairs, but has an elevator, the stairs are not a big issue. The problem is when stairs with no risers are the only way to get to your front door.

RECOMMENDED READING

FENG SHUI BOOKS

Design & Feng Shui: Logos, Trademarks & Signboards by Evelyn Lip is the only book of its kind. Ms. Lip is an architect and she's brilliant! This book covers *everything* related to the graphic presentation of your store.

Sarah Rossbach is one of my favorite feng shui authors. Page 82 of her *Living Color* has an excellent chart for choosing the **interior color** for bookstores, galleries, card shops, music stores, pharmacies, food stores, clothing stores, computer stores, jewelry stores, wine shops, furniture stores, toy stores, and more.

Just as I was finishing the book that you are holding, I came across *Feng Shui for Retailers* by Linda Cahan. It's very different from this book. Cahan's specialty is visual merchandizing and store design. Her author referrals are all top-notch. I bought my copy directly from the publisher, ST Media Group, whom I *highly* recommend for books on retail design. But the cover design has too much *black* (yin) on the entire cover. Such a book gets lost on bookstore shelves.

OFFICE FENG SHUI

Office feng shui books abound, but most deal with cardinal directions, which are not used in the Landform School Feng Shui that I practice. That being said, these two books stand out:

- *Feng Shui for Business & Office* is by Jes Lim, one of my favorite feng shui writers. Huge sections of this book have nothing to do with the compass directions and instead contain a rare bounty of feng shi wisdom, much of it found nowhere else in English. It's very clearly illustrated.
- Raphael Simons' *Feng Shui Strategies for Business Success* has several small but excellent sections. Pages 171-175 succinctly cover the two back corners, which I often call the power corners. Desk arrangement is explained on pages 179 & 180.

RETAIL BOOKS

Often the owner of a store starts managing other people without ever having studied how to be a good manager. Do yourself and your employees a favor by *at least skimming* through a few popular management books. They're popular because they help people manipulate other people's behavior. That's what you're doing—manipulating the behavior of your sales team so that they properly represent your store. Your employees should be polite, helpful, enthusiastic people. Learn to train them to be that way. Most popular management books are written for office situations, not for retail stores in particular. Just skip those sections and read the parts that apply to *your situations* with employees. And skip the long stories that tell how some particular business did something. Those stories are often eighty percent of the book. Look for the gist of it, the statement of the principle at issue. *Some* of those principles will make you a better manager. And one or two good new ideas are well worth the time to educate yourself in what you're doing every day. You're a busy person, so I'll direct you to specific pages in some of the books.

The One-Minute Manager by Blanchard and Johnson has two excellent pages (44 & 59) explaining positive reprimanding as well as praising—both should be done *immediately* when the opportunity arises (but *not in front of customers*, I will add). Every store manager must delegate, and usually the more the better. You and every manager in your store should read the section on "Strategies for Delegating Effectively" in Michael LeBoeuf's *Working Smart: How to Accomplish More in Half the Time.* Those six pages are quite an education, as is the one page on "Guidelines for Working at a Desk." He ends that section with this: "Few of us do our best work with a heavily cluttered and disorganized desk." That's very basic feng shui.

Why We Buy by Paco Underhill never mentions the words "chi energy" but that's what the book is all about. This whole book is a must-read! *Inside the Mind of the Shopper: The Science of Retailing* by Herb Sorensen is another must-read book. If that subject is fascinating to you (as it is to me) then take a look at *How We Decide* by Jonah Lehrer. It's not particularly about retail; it's about how our brains make decisions. *Why People Buy Things They Don't Need: Understanding and predicting Consumer Behavior* by Pamela Danziger lists categories of merchandise, then explains why people buy items within those categories. *The New Rules of Retail* by Robert Lewis and Michael Dart offers an interesting perspective on retail during the last 150 years and where it's heading. It is, however, completely focused on the super-big national and international chain stores. (The bigger they are, the harder they fall.) The authors have no real retail experience except for consulting. It's a different story with *Retail Success!* by George Whalin. He spent 25 years as a retailer before becoming a consultant, and even if I don't agree with every word, *Retail Success!* is by far **the most relevant book** that I'm recommending to you.

Transactions end in a yang (positive) direction when a sale happens and everyone is happy. When a transaction goes off into a yin direction—ending in a way perceived as negative by the customer—it's not good for your store. Page 143 of *Hey, I'm the Customer* by Ron Willingham explains the power of turning a customer off: "The average 'wronged' customer will tell 8 to 16 people. (More than 10 percent will tell 20 people.)" "Ninety-one percent of unhappy customers will never purchase goods or services from you again." "If you make an effort to remedy customers' complaints, 82 to 95 percent will stay with you." "It costs five times as much to attract a new customer as it costs to keep an old one." If you have to solve customer problems, you must be good at moving even difficult transactions in a positive direction. Read pages 146 & 147 and you will quickly understand the *causes* of most of your customer service problems.

Good Service Is Good Business by Catherine Devrye isn't solely about retail situations—but much of the book is, and it contains many gems such as this: "70 percent of customers are satisfied if they only need to deal with one employee to fix their complaint. If a second person is involved, the satisfaction rate drops to 61 percent." Devrye is a spunky writer and judging from her stories, she's also a spunky customer. I love her section "Say Yes Instead of No."

The fifteen-page section "The Ten Commandments of Service," in *Lead or Get Off the Pot* by Pat Croce, is a super-fast read when you skip the stories. It's a quick refresher, or something to show your employees.

The best book for deciding the name of a store is *POP: Stand Out in Any Crowd* by Sam Horn. I rave about it in the first paragraph in Chapter One. I don't, however, think that her advice on spelling names uniquely is good for retail stores.

You've undoubtedly noticed that in this book I've occasionally stressed the importance of using specific words. Words matter greatly. They can tilt an interaction into a yang direction (positive—best for stores) or a yin direction (negative—not good for stores). Whole books have been devoted to using specific words in business. You don't have to read the books in their entirety, but do read the pages and sections that I've noted. Hopefully you don't feel the need to lie, but the 20-page chapter on lying in *The Gentle Art of Verbal Self-Defense for Business Success* by Suzette Elgin is something that every owner or manager should read. *Tongue Fu!* by Sam Horn (who also wrote *POP* from the previous paragraph) is not written specifically for business, but has occasional framed pages with "Words to Use, Word to Lose." This part of the book can be read very quickly and if you are curious you can then read in depth.

Business Etiquette: 101 Ways to Conduct Business with Charm and Savvy by Ann Marie Sabath is wonderful and easy to read. Everyone I've shown this book to has been quite impressed with it. Like most business books it is concerned with office situations, but very many of those situations occur in retail. You'll probably say (as I did), "I wish I'd had this book sooner."

The number one book on organizing is *Getting Things Done*

by David Allen. It's a *must-read* for accomplishing your goals and objectives.

And sooner or later we have to write words on paper, even in this computer-centric world. *Change Your Handwriting, Change Your Life* by Vimala Rodgers is about the energy of handwriting. Just as you can change your life by moving your stuff around according to feng shui principles, you can also change your life by altering how you form the letters of the words that you write. It's the feng shui of handwriting and it's very common sense and powerful.

GLOSSARY

BAGUA MIRROR

Bagua mirrors represent perfect balance and harmony. But they should not be used casually. Don't use them for decoration because their purpose is protection. In my own practice, I almost never recommend them for indoor use, and never to *attract* energy. They're the strongest solution used in feng shui when a problem is particularly onerous. They are used symbolically to *push energy away*, and at the same time put things back in perfect order. A feng shui bagua mirror is specific, in that it has eight sides and is decorated with the eight *I Ching* trigrams. Some feng shui consultants prefer bagua mirrors that have frames with red, green and golden colors. If there's a blue plastic film covering the glass, be sure to peel it off when putting up the mirror.

The concave shape is often recommended for outside because of its ability to *shrink* problems. In a concave mirror a distant image looks very small. When some feng shui professionals recommend bagua mirrors for outside use, they recommend the concave kind almost exclusively. There are also many uses for convex bagua mirrors, such as to push back the harsh energy of a highway. There's a photograph of a bagua mirror at the end of Chapter 2.

A Seal of Solomon mirror has the traditional symbol of two equilateral triangles, which represents perfect balance. It can feel culturally more appropriate to some people than a bagua mirror, and can be used anytime a bagua mirror is called for. One of the virtues of these mirrors is that you can make one yourself—just be sure to get the proportions correct. A source for nice stained glass ones is in Sources. The use of Seal-of-Solomon mirrors is innovative in feng shui. For more information on this, read *Feng Shui & Your Health* by Jes Lim.

CHI ENERGY

Chi refers to energy—of any kind. It's also spelled qi in Pinyin, and ki in Japanese. If chi is negative or harsh, it's called sha chi or shar chi.

CURES

Cures, solutions, or remedies are what to do when a feng shui problem is noted. There are two kinds of cures:

Real

A real solution really does change the situation.

Symbolic

A symbolic solution is what is used when a real cure is not feasible. State your intention out loud when installing a symbolic cure.

Smudging (with Sage)

If the place is physically dirty, do a thorough, detailed cleaning of the entire space in conjunction with the vibrational cleansing. Preferably do the physical cleaning first. Do it during the day, and have every window open as fully as possible. Let the natural breezes do some of the work for you.

Walk the entire inside perimeter of each room, including closets. Go in a clockwise direction, which means turning to your left as soon as you have entered the room. Carry burning sage incense or a sage smudge stick. If you can manage it, carry a pure-sounding bell, and ring it every few steps. If someone is assisting you, one can carry the incense, and the other can carry the bell.

If no bell is readily available, don't worry: you were born with the right tool—use your hands and clap. Don't clap as if you were applauding. Do single, loud, sharp claps when you get to corners and doorways and any place that feels a little unusual—any kind of unusual. It is an extremely powerful, assertive thing to do. You are using your own hands to claim your rightful ownership of a space. It works oh-so-well! Clap high and clap low. There is no way that you can clap and hold incense at the same time, so if you are doing this alone, you will have to make two complete circuits.

Sing, chant, or speak aloud—whichever you are most comfortable with. The ancient chant "Om" is always good. Absolutely anything that expresses your intention is appropriate. You could simply say, "Peace to this space," over and over. Your voice should be assertive and rather loud. Don't worry about the neighbors. This is most likely to be a one-time occurrence, and even if they can hear you, they'll get over it.

Make sure the smoke from the incense wafts high and low.

Bring the incense near the floor and the ceiling, in every corner, including closets and cabinets. Do an ultra-thorough job. It's okay if it takes a while. You are not going to be doing it every day.

Sage smudging is called for when a store is first opening, when it has been robbed, or after the dismissal of a problem employee. The process is sometimes called clearing. Sage smudge sticks are readily available; if you prefer to use sage incense, the best I know of is from Juniper Ridge. See Sources.

Yin/Yang

Yin and yang are the components of an ancient system for dividing energy (chi) into two categories, with nothing being totally yang and nothing being totally yin. This system is discussed in the book *Primitive Classification* by Durkheim and Mauss who say, "Such classifications are thus intended, above all, to connect ideas, to unify knowledge; as such, they may be said without inexactitude to be scientific, and to constitute a first philosophy of nature." The yin/yang symbolizes a very basic concept—balance—a balance that changes, but stays balanced.

The yin/yang system is for categorizing energy and things, not *judging* good or bad. However, the Retail Yin/Yang Chart in the Introduction should definitely be used for deciding what is best for *a store*, where yang energy should predominate. I'm including the following chart to give you an idea of how the yin/yang concept can be used in other applications. Life isn't *all* about your store, and it shouldn't be.

Non-Retail Yin/Yang Chart

Here are some general concepts (that *don't* apply to retail stores) divided into yang and yin:

Yang	**Yin**
Male, Masculine	Female, Feminine
Up, Upper	Down, Lower
Dry	Wet or Moist
Fire	Water
Vertical	Horizontal
Young	Old
Loud	Silent or Quiet
Hot	Cold
Hard	Soft
Outdoors	Indoors
Few things	Many things
Slick	Textured

Sources

If you have need of these items *and don't have local sources,* here are some suggestions. Several of these sources have wholesale policies if you'd like to carry their products in you store.

Gaussmeters

Alphalab, 800-658-7030, www.trifield.com

They sell gaussmeters for measuring EMFs – electromagnetic fields. I've owned their Trifield meter for years. It's relatively expensive, but I've seen other brands on Amazon for as little as $30. Electromagnetic radiation is invisible but quite real and measurable. More people should own gaussmeters, so that they can show friends, family, and coworkers what they are being exposed to.

Tiny Wind chimes

Karizma, 415-861-4515, karizma1@att.net

An excellent source for tiny wind chimes.

BAGUA MIRRORS

If there's not a Chinatown or Chinese dry goods store in your area, try eBay for a good selection and a wide range of prices. There's a picture of a bagua mirror at the end of Chapter 2.

SEAL-OF-SOLOMON MIRRORS

Lavender Moon Gallery, 808-324-7708, lavendermoongallery. com

The mirrors represent perfect balance and are designed by Dianne McMillen. The mirrors are surrounded by stained glass lotus frames in a choice of colors—very beautiful.

SAGE

Juniper Ridge, 800-205-9499, juniperridge.com

They have *excellent* sage incense for clearing. Incense is easier to handle and less messy than using a sage smudge wand or bundle.

CRYSTALS

Xinacat Prisms and Crystal Jewelry, http://stores.shop.ebay.com/XinaCat-Prisms-and-Crystal-Jewelry

This is an eBay store with an excellent selection of crystals at decent prices. It's a good place to get the *best* clear octagonal crystals—ones that create large bands of color when placed in the sunlight.

MOLDING FOR GLASS EDGES

brandsport.com, 877-341-6555

They have a 3/8 inch auto trim molding intended for the edges of car doors. The application is a very simple peel-and-stick, and it works perfectly to cover bare glass edges. It comes in sixty colors, including many metallics and five different whites. The specific page that has the L-shaped flexible molding is:

http://www.brandsport.com/3-8-molding.html

METALLIC PAINT

Modern Masters metallic paint from Cox Paint, 310-393-7208

This is a very high quality metallic paint that comes in a large array of colors. It is not simple to apply.

The specific web page is: http://www.coxpaint.com/store/cart.php?target=category&category_id=260

METALLIC WALLPAPER

Cavalier Wall Liner, 800-221-5798

The specific web page is: http://www.wallliner.com/metallic.html

INDEX

ACKNOWLEDGEMENTS

Steve Mann has helped immensely, both in my life and with all my books. I also thank Susan Levitt. Her expertise and her willingness to share it have been a great blessing.

ABOUT THE AUTHOR

Clear Englebert began working in retail at Montgomery Ward in Huntsville, Alabama when he was fifteen. Still a teenager, he became manager of the paperback department of Bookland's largest store. At nineteen, he opened his first Huntsville bookstore, called A Good Book Store. In 1978, Clear founded Books as Seeds, and in 1989, Opening Books (a 501c3 library and gift shop). He has managed at Green Apple Books  (San Francisco's largest independent bookstore), at Pearly Gates Natural Foods in Huntsville, and at Ohana O Ka `Aina Natural Foods in Kona, Hawaii.

With decades of experience in retail visual merchandizing, Clear began a career as a feng shui consultant in Hawaii in 1995.

He moved to San Francisco in 1996 to further his feng shui education. His first best-selling book, *Feng Shui Demystified*, was originally published in 2000 and was followed the next year with *Bedroom Feng Shui*. They have appeared in four languages and, after a decade, have been reissued in revised and expanded editions. Clear teaches feng shui in Hawaii and California and consults on homes, gardens, and commercial spaces.

If you have a retail store and would like to sell these books, they can be ordered through Ingram Distributors or Baker & Taylor at a 40% discount (fully returnable) or they can be ordered at a 48% discount from iUniverse—Media Mail being the most affordable shipping option. The contact information for ordering from iUniverse is 800-288-4677 (phone), 812-339-6554 (fax), or channelsales@authorsolutions.com.

Clear has written two Hawaii feng shui books: *Feng Shui for Hawaii* (2008) and *Feng Shui for Hawaii Gardens* (2012). They are also available from Ingram Distributing or direct from Watermark Publishing at 866-900-2665.

Clear's website is fungshway.com.